Conservation Heroes

STEVE and BINDI IRWIN

Conservation Heroes

Conservation Heroes

STEVE and BINDI IRWIN

Amy Breguet

CHELSEA HOUSE
An Infobase Learning Company

Steve and Bindi Irwin

Copyright ©2011 by Infobase Learning

All rights reserved. No part of this book may be reproduced or utilized in
any form or by any means, electronic or mechanical, including photocopying,
recording, or by any information storage or retrieval systems, without permission
in writing from the publisher. For information, contact:

Chelsea House
An imprint of Infobase Learning
132 West 31st Street
New York, NY 10001

Library of Congress Cataloging-in-Publication Data
Breguet, Amy.
   Steve and Bindi Irwin / by Amy Breguet.
      p. cm. — (Conservation heroes)
   Includes bibliographical references and index.
   ISBN 978-1-60413-957-0 (hardcover)
      1. Irwin, Steve, 1962–2006. 2. Irwin, Bindi, 1998–   3. Herpetologists—
Australia—Biography. 4. Naturalists—Australia—Biography. 5. Wildlife
conservationists—Australia—Biography. I. Title. II. Series.
   QL31.I78B74 2010
   333.95′4160922—dc22

                                                                 2010028919

Chelsea House books are available at special discounts when purchased in
bulk quantities for businesses, associations, institutions, or sales promotions.
Please call our Special Sales Department in New York at (212) 967-8800 or
(800) 322-8755.

You can find Chelsea House on the World Wide Web
at http://www.chelseahouse.com.

Text design by Annie O'Donnell
Cover design by Takeshi Takahashi
Composition by Newgen
Cover printed by Yurchak Printing, Landisville, Pa.
Book printed and bound by Yurchak Printing, Landisville, Pa.
Date printed: April 2011
Printed in the United States of America

10 9 8 7 6 5 4 3 2 1

This book is printed on acid-free paper.

All links and Web addresses were checked and verified to be correct at the time
of publication. Because of the dynamic nature of the Web, some addresses and
links may have changed since publication and may no longer be valid.

Contents

The Family that Catches Crocs Together

You know that the Irwin family just is different. Let's face it, how many families wake up in the morning and go, "Let's introduce our children and our friends and our family [to] and work with wildlife. . . ." That's natural; that's a family thing.

—Terri Irwin

It's a place most would call the middle of nowhere, this remote strip of wooded wetland somewhere in the Outback. Terri Irwin, whose husband, Steve, is leading an eager team of croc-catchers-in-training through the area, has a far more enthusiastic description for what is actually a corner of Queensland's Lakefield National Park. "[We're in] one of the most important conservation strongholds of both the saltwater crocodile and the Australian freshwater croc," she says in a voice-over for this 2004 episode of the Irwins' *Crocodile Hunter Diaries*. Then, in a welcome summary for the less nature-savvy, she adds: "This is serious crocodile country."

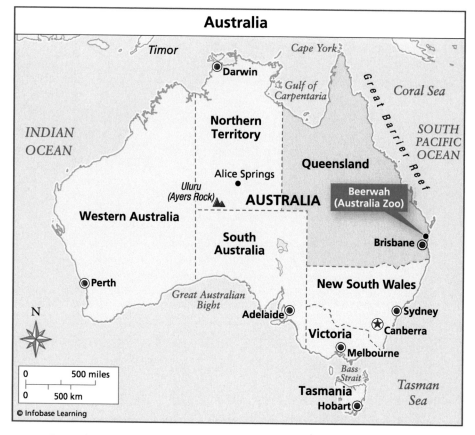

Australia Zoo is located on Steve Irwin Way in Beerwah, which is in the Australian state of Queensland.

Having power-napped on the long plane ride in from civilization, Terri is more than ready to help the Crocodile Hunter—as Steve has been widely known for nearly seven years at this point—on this exciting and important venture. In partnership with the Queensland Parks and Wildlife Service of the Australian government, Steve, Terri, and their assistants, representing the Irwins' Australia Zoo, plan to trap many of these two species of crocodile and take them away.

Croc-napping? It may seem so, but this project is far from either criminal or cruel. On the contrary, the Irwins' mission is to rescue these crocodiles from a probable deadly fate. Development of territories previously inhabited only by wildlife has made crocodiles a long-threatened species, even endangered in some areas. By relocating the reptiles to natural human-free zones or bringing them back to the zoo, the Irwin group will help preserve one of the world's only prehistoric creatures.

Having reached a spot near, but not too near, a crocodile-infested river, the group begins to set up camp—and traps. Terri explains to viewers that the team uses both a floating aluminum trap and a soft mesh trap on land. A crocodile, unaware that someone just wants to help, might be suspicious of a large black structure on the water and might be more likely to go toward the less conspicuous land trap. In this way, the trappers have their bases covered.

The trapping drill is nothing new for Steve and Terri, for whom crocodile hunting has been a way of married life from day one. For Steve himself, the vocation goes back much farther, since being raised on the grounds of his family's reptile park. Still, no two adventures are ever alike; every crocodile-saving mission is something new, something unpredictable, something thrilling, and this particular project is something downright special. It's special because joining the advanced students today is a new assistant, someone who has never experienced a real crocodile hunt firsthand before. She helps with camp setup and inspection of the traps. "You reckon this trap will work all right?" Steve asks her. Since this is her first crocodile hunt, though, he leaves the more dangerous parts of the process to the pros.

Before long, a crocodile has entered the mesh land trap, just on the river's edge. The advanced students are immediately on the scene, holding ropes taut while Steve wrangles the animal and secures a noose around its snout. The team then pulls the crocodile away from the water and prepares to transport it to safety. With team members restraining the enmeshed crocodile securely from end to end, it's the young assistant's opportunity to get involved. Steve calls her over and orders her to help hold the tail. As she quickly approaches, he sees that his small-statured student is ready

Terri and Steve Irwin playfully pose with daughter Bindi and a stuffed crocodile in this July 2002 photo. A year later, Bindi had her first contact with a real, wild crocodile.

and willing to help—but apparently not willing to drop everything to do it.

"Can you eat your sandwich and hang on to that tail?" he asks the young lady, whose preschool-aged peers would surely love to see her now.

"Yeah," comes her mumbled assurance.

"All right," Steve replies casually and continues. After all, he maybe reasons, a multitasker can only be an asset.

The newest team member, of course, is Steve's own daughter, Bindi Sue. At only five years of age, she has just made her first-ever contact with a wild crocodile—and the moment has been captured for the world to see.

SOMETHING TO BE PROUD OF

In Queensland, Australia, the Irwin name had been synonymous with wildlife rescue since before Steve was born. His parents, Bob and Lyn, were both avidly involved with the cause. "My parents and my environment molded me to be who I am," Steve told the *Worcester Telegram and Gazette* in 2002, "and then they helped me blossom, go past that, because they knew I had an instinct." Later, when fate brought together the future TV star and the American girl whose animal-loving soul perfectly matched his, it seemed inevitable that any children the couple might have would inherit their passion. Within a few years, the first child arrived, and that theory was confirmed. At just two weeks old, Bindi Irwin reached out in wonder to touch nonvenomous snakes and posed comfortably for a photo with a friendly brown tarantula on her head. From there, it had been one animal adventure after another—such is the lucky life of a crocodile hunter's kid. But when, out in the Australian wilderness, she put her own two small hands on this iconic reptile, it was as if Bindi Sue Irwin had taken a torch.

The crocodile, it's no surprise, is arguably the animal whose relationship with the family goes back the farthest. The efforts that would earn Steve his honorary title essentially began as a father-son operation in the early 1970s, when Steve was just a child himself. Saving these widely feared creatures eventually became so important to the Irwins that they founded International Crocodile Rescue (ICR), a major zoo project devoted to crocodile conservation—which ICR emphasizes means much more than removing or otherwise physically protecting the animals. "Catching a problem crocodile is only half the problem," Steve wrote on the history page of the volunteer organization's Web site. "The educational follow-up is equally as important . . . . We have no doubt that it is possible to change the general public's perception of these important animals from one of fear to one where its presence in an area is embraced as something to be proud of."

Fear of crocodiles is something Steve and Terri's own children seemingly have never even known. "No, I love them," Bindi answered in January 2007 when CNN TV host Larry King asked if she was afraid of crocodiles. "They're the sweetest, most beautiful animals on the face of this earth." Then she added, "Everything is."

BEYOND CROCODILES

Whether speaking of Steve's family of origin or the one in which he was "Dad," this much is certain: If it's in the interest of wildlife, it's

MODERN-DAY DINOSAURS

Few animals have seen the coming and going of both the Tyrannosaurus Rex and the second millennium A.D. But crocodiles have, and for that alone, conservationists say they deserve some respect. Here are some facts about these living links to Earth's past:

- Although experts often refer to these ancient creatures as "modern-day dinosaurs," crocodiles actually descend from *archosaurs,* an order of animals that outdates the known dinosaurs.
- *Crocodilian* refers to the order of animals that includes the crocodile and its U.S.-dwelling cousin, the alligator. Of the 23 crocodilian species, about half are endangered or threatened by humans.
- Crocodiles are native to Australia, Mexico, South America, Central America, Africa, and Southeast Asia.
- Most at home in or around swamps and slow-moving rivers, crocodiles can hold their breath underwater for over an hour.
- Strict carnivores, crocodiles will eat essentially any animal they can grab off the banks, from birds and frogs

of interest to the Irwins. "I consider myself a wildlife warrior," Steve told the Australian newspaper *The Age* in 2003. "My mission is to save the world's endangered species." A mission like that is going to require attention to a lot more than the plight of the crocodiles— and the Irwins readily give it.

The family has launched, or helped launch, countless wildlife conservation efforts over the years. Privately and through Australia Zoo, they have purchased hundreds of thousands of acres of land in

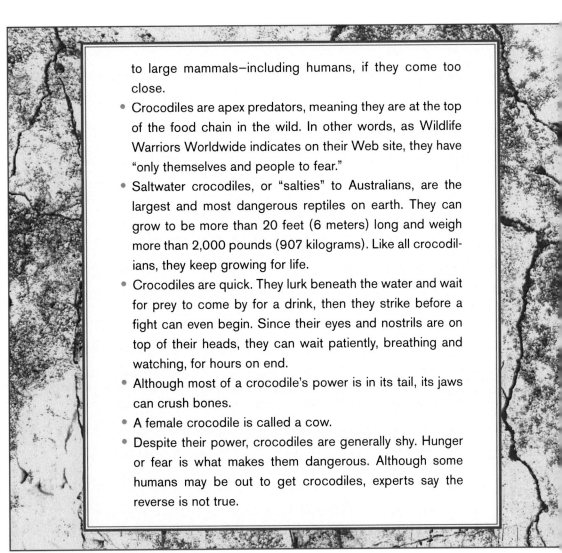

to large mammals—including humans, if they come too close.

- Crocodiles are apex predators, meaning they are at the top of the food chain in the wild. In other words, as Wildlife Warriors Worldwide indicates on their Web site, they have "only themselves and people to fear."
- Saltwater crocodiles, or "salties" to Australians, are the largest and most dangerous reptiles on earth. They can grow to be more than 20 feet (6 meters) long and weigh more than 2,000 pounds (907 kilograms). Like all crocodilians, they keep growing for life.
- Crocodiles are quick. They lurk beneath the water and wait for prey to come by for a drink, then they strike before a fight can even begin. Since their eyes and nostrils are on top of their heads, they can wait patiently, breathing and watching, for hours on end.
- Although most of a crocodile's power is in its tail, its jaws can crush bones.
- A female crocodile is called a cow.
- Despite their power, crocodiles are generally shy. Hunger or fear is what makes them dangerous. Although some humans may be out to get crocodiles, experts say the reverse is not true.

several countries with the sole purpose of protecting these natural habitats from human interference. The zoo itself also runs individualized programs for the protection and care of endangered or threatened species, including koalas, tigers, elephants, cheetahs, and giant land tortoises. Steve was once the face for the Australian Quarantine and Inspection Service, and Terri, Bindi, and the couple's son, Bob, are at the forefront of the fight to save the whales. Every day, the family continues to demonstrate that a wildlife conservationist's job is never done.

What Steve and Terri realized early in their partnership is the key to doing the job effectively. They would invite the public to join them in the wilderness—without leaving the comfort of their own homes.

INTO PEOPLE'S HEARTS

Any effort's strength is in its numbers, and the Irwins needed to get conservation into the consciousness of as many people as possible. But they knew they wouldn't succeed by appealing to minds alone. "If you can't get wilds into people's hearts," Steve told Larry King in a 2005 interview, "then we haven't got a hope in heck of saving them because people don't want to save something they don't know." This is the very reason why Australia Zoo had become what it had, a place where the public could come to see, hear, and learn about many amazing creatures. This was an invaluable start, but they needed more.

Steve had already captured countless crocodile-trapping quests on film, thanks to his dad, who had sent him a video camera when the 20-something Steve was off on a solo mission for the Queensland government. After Steve's friend and documentary filmmaker John Stainton saw the amateur footage, which showed not only wild crocodiles but Steve's dynamic communication both with and about them, the rest was quickly history. "Irwin was the modern-day embodiment of the television underwater explorers of the 1950s and 1960s," read Irwin's obituary in the British newspaper *The Independent.* The reference was to the legendary

"THE CAMERA LOVED HIM"

When Australian filmmaker John Stainton needed to feature a creature, he'd turn to the continent's favorite animal park. He'd employ not only Australia Zoo's animals but also their skilled and spirited handler, Steve Irwin, who would assist on commercial shoots that required lizards, turtles, and the like. Then in 1990, a client of John's envisioned a commercial that would require a bit more. A guy would toss a beer across a river to another guy, and the second guy would save the hurtling beverage just before a suddenly emerging crocodile could snatch it. When he pitched the idea to Steve, he was game but under one condition: that it be his hand in front of the croc's jaws. It was a deal.

John filmed the commercial at the zoo, marking the first time that he had used the location. The scene—starring two actors, Steve's hand, and Monty the saltie—went off without a hitch. So, when Steve handed John a collection of VHS tapes showing adventures he'd recorded while hunting and catching crocodiles, the seasoned cinematographer was certainly willing to take a look. Alone in the Outback, Steve had been producer, crew, and talent, propping the camera in trees or sticking it in patches of mud. On popping the tapes into his VCR back home in South Brisbane, John could not believe what he saw. "It was three hours of captivating film and I watched it straight through, twice," John told Terri for her 2007 memoir *Steve & Me.* "It was Steve. The camera loved him."

John knew he had something unique on his hands, and Australian TV producers agreed. They gave him the go-ahead to document the crocodile hunter's adventures himself. Appropriately titled *The Crocodile Hunter,* the resulting program aired in Australia in 1996 and, by 1999, had reached viewers in more than 130 countries.

(continues)

Saltwater crocodiles, nicknamed "salties," are the largest of all living reptiles, and a large population of the species thrives in northern Australia. The largest saltie ever found was 23 feet (7 meters) long.

(continued)

Steve was pleased to realize that he possessed a flair for much more than reading about and wrangling animals. This newly discovered skill would help him to accomplish the one thing he literally lived for. "I've got the ability to be attractive to wildlife and vice versa," he told interviewer Larry King in 2004. "Then, on top of that, I've got a gift that I didn't know I had, of communicating to cameras, which is in essence looking to millions of people. Combine those two and there you see my mission is to educate people about conservation." Worldwide fame, it seems, was just icing on the cake.

John has also worked with the Irwins on several *Crocodile Hunter* spinoffs and specials for Animal Planet, including *Croc Files, The Crocodile Hunter Diaries, New Breed Vets,* and *My Daddy, the Crocodile Hunter.*

Jacques Cousteau—naturally an idol of Steve's—and Austrian environmentalist couple Lotte and Hans Hass, whose deep-sea endeavors had made both the big and small screens. Thus, from the depths of the sea to the depths of the wilderness, from traditional documentary to crazy *crocumentary,* TV as a wildlife conservation medium was back—and, some might argue, better than ever before.

A NEW CROC CATCHER

Back in "serious crocodile country" on that memorable day of training, cameras have just recorded Bindi's symbolic anointment as her dad's croc-catching protégé. Steve facilitated the moment by having Bindi grab the tail of a crocodile that he and his students had just captured and secured—marking her first-ever contact with a wild croc. Now he gently lifts his daughter and stands her in front of the team, with whom she has some important information to share. "Just so you guys know," she tells her fellow wranglers, who are still holding tight, "a croc strikes from the tail up to the legs, all the way up to the mouth." Everyone graciously thanks her for the valuable tip.

The crocodile, of course, harms no one, but five-year-old Bindi clearly has been bitten nonetheless—by the wildlife-loving bug. She's ready to embrace what Terri, in *Steve & Me,* calls the Irwin family motto: "The family that catches crocs together, rocks together." Even when unspeakable tragedy later threatens to tear them apart, this is a family who will, remarkably, rock on.

Steve's Early Years: Animals Everywhere

That was absolutely the most incredible time of my entire life, for me, my dad and my family—running around up in north Queensland catching all these crocodiles.

—Steve Irwin

"Chip off the old croc" is the wordplay *People* magazine uses in a 2007 article to aptly describe Bindi Irwin. The phrase, perfect for the famous crocodile hunter's daughter, could also apply to the crocodile hunter himself. Steve Irwin's love of modern-day dinosaurs and all other creatures began with his own parents, literally in his own backyard.

A NATURAL MATCH

Life in the early 1940s was not easy for many. Families worldwide had suffered the impact of the Great Depression, a historical economic crisis triggered largely by a devastating stock market crash in 1929. Although countries began to recover within a few years of the crash, it took many people well over a decade to find financial security again. It was an especially difficult era for families like young Robert Eric Irwin's of Victoria, Australia, for whom the Great Depression was only the first blow. Soon after, both Robert's father and his grandfather—Steve Irwin's grandfather and great-grandfather—were killed while fighting in Southeast Asia during World War II. Robert's mother was left to raise him and his brother alone in the Dandenong Ranges of Victoria.

In the nearby town of Boronia, there lived a young lady named Lynette "Lyn" Hakainsson, who met Robert—known by most everyone as Bob—when they were both children. Lyn's father had also fought in the war, but in an ultimately lucky twist of fate, he had been injured and returned home safely. Bob and Lyn became friends, and before Lyn had even said goodbye to her teens, the two had decided to spend their lives together. When they married, she was 18 and a maternity nurse, and he was a 20-year-old successful plumber. They settled in Essendon, a suburb of Melbourne, and their "wild" adventure began.

They were both very good at their jobs, but perhaps even more important to them was the off-hours interest they shared: the rescue, study, and care of wild animals. For Lyn, it wasn't so far a cry from her paid vocation, as someone who chooses to help bring babies into the world is likely to have a knack for nurturing. For Bob's part, wildlife, particularly the cold-blooded type, had simply been a natural part of his world since childhood. In the 2001 book *The Crocodile Hunter,* Steve credits his grandmother Marjorie (Bob's mother) for imparting on her sons an appreciation for "the Australian bush and its reptiles."

Given their mutual passion, it seemed the nature-loving newlyweds' homestead was bound to become more than just a family dwelling. Within a few short years, the place would, in fact, be filled with the laughter of three children . . . among other lively sounds.

THE GREATEST GIFTS OF ALL

The notably close bond between Lyn and her only son, Steven Robert Irwin, began the day he was born—two decades to the day after her own birth. "I was born right fair smack on my Mum's 20th birthday," Steve wrote on the official Crocodile Hunter Web site. "Crikey! A birthday present she'll never forget." It was February 22, 1962, and the Irwins had just welcomed their second child. Daughter Joy had arrived not long before, and a second daughter, Mandy, soon completed the family of five—that is, of course, if you count only the people. Between Lyn's injured and orphaned mammals and Bob's lizards and snakes, the Irwins had a regular menagerie at their Essendon home. "There were [animals] everywhere," Irwin's childhood neighbor, Tony Piscitelli, told the South Australian newspaper *The Adelaide Advertiser* in 2006. "Steve had an old pool out in the backyard. He had taken all the water out of it and filled it with sand and had reptiles living in there. Dad thought he was always a little crazy. He was, I suppose."

Young Steve had reason to take pride in caring for these animals that lived in this pool-turned-sanctuary; he had helped his dad catch them. Inspired by their son's obvious interest and sense of responsibility with the family's rescued brood, Lyn and Bob wanted to give Steve an unforgettable birthday present of his own. When he turned six, he became the proud owner of a 12-foot-long (3.6-meter-long) scrub python, which he named Fred. The budding herpetologist (someone who studies reptiles) was thrilled with the unique gift, even if he didn't get to experience one particular joy that usually comes with a new pet—he wasn't allowed to play with it. If he had, Steve explained in *The Crocodile Hunter,* the snake might have mistaken its relatively small owner for a meal.

Although there's no question that Steve inherited his dad's herpetology gene, he shared his mom's softer side as well—softer and furrier, one might say. Bob actively sought and saved the scalier creatures as Lyn, true to her maternal nature, housed, fed, cuddled, and cured countless baby mammals. "People tend to focus just on the reptiles, but if you can imagine that in my house at any one given time I was being raised with a dozen joey kangaroos," Steve told *Reader's Digest Australia.* "My mum would set up chairs like this with fake pouches—you know, marsupials, marsupial pouches—and she had to become their mum, well actually we did, you know so I was bottle-feeding joey kangaroos like every night of my life and that was normal. It was completely normal. We had possums running through the roof, you know Mum raised up sugar gliders and, you know, wombats and koalas running through the house, yeah it wasn't just all snakes and things that can kill you. It really wasn't."

The "snakes and things," however, would be at the center of the Irwins' next major endeavor. It was time to invite the public to see these amazing creatures up close, to take that first step toward opening the public's eyes to wildlife conservation. It was time to pack up the growing family and head north.

A WALK IN THE PARK

The Irwins' unusual sense of comfort with living among animals was something Steve stressed time and again in interviews. In the *Reader's Digest* article, he went on to say that "what seems bizarre and dangerous and hard-hitting [to most people] is just like a walk in the park to me. I don't know any other way." Officially, that walk in the park began in the early 1970s.

The year Steve turned eight, Bob, Lyn, their kids, and their creatures moved to a 4-acre (1.6-hectare) plot of land in Queensland, the Australian state that occupies the continent's northeastern corner. Located largely in a tropical zone, coastal Queensland enjoys a lot of warm, sunny weather, making it the perfect place for the couple to realize a longtime dream. In April 1973, the Irwins opened the Beerwah Reptile Park, the humble attraction that would, over two decades, evolve into the world-famous Australia Zoo. It had taken a full three years of hard work to make the place ready for the public. The first reptile to officially take up residence at the park, which soon housed everything from tree snakes to giant crocodiles, was none other than Fred, the scrub python.

Building a reptile park meant lots of preparation of the property, but it required plenty of field work as well. It was this second part

FROM PYTHON TO PANTHEON: AN AUSTRALIA ZOO TIMELINE

When Fred the scrub python took up residence at the young reptile park where he was the only reptile (and only resident, at that), he couldn't have known what his home would one day become. Here's a summary of events from the birth of the Beerwah Reptile Park to the extraordinary Australia Zoo of today:

1970: Bob and Lyn Irwin buy 4 acres (1.6 hectares) on the Sunshine Coast of Queensland and move their family there from Victoria.

1970–1973: The Irwins work tirelessly to build their dream of a reptile park, preparing the property and catching countless breeds of reptiles in the wild.

April 1973: The gates of the Beerwah Reptile Park open to the public.

1980: The Irwins purchase an additional 4 acres (1.6 hectares) to expand the park, which they rename the Queensland Reptile and Fauna Park.

1987: The Crocodile Environmental Park, which Bob and Steve created to help protect saltwater crocodiles, opens on the newer half of the property.

1991: Steve takes over management of the Queensland Reptile and Fauna Park.

that had father and son frequenting the wild as they searched for reptiles to take out of harm's way and into the safety of the park. In some cases, the service they performed was not only for the animals and the Irwins' own park but also for the national government. The

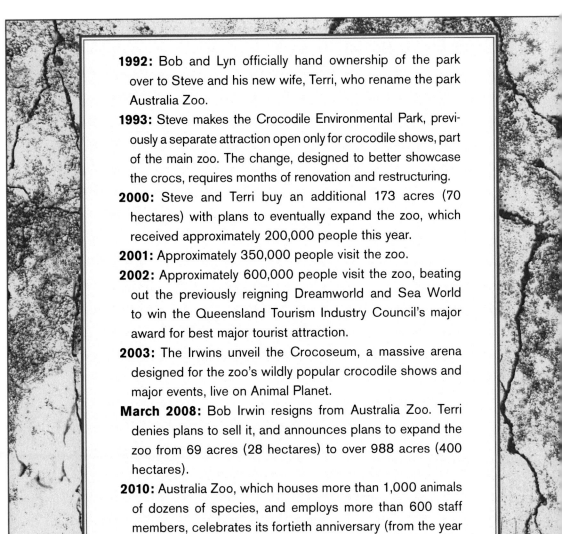

1992: Bob and Lyn officially hand ownership of the park over to Steve and his new wife, Terri, who rename the park Australia Zoo.

1993: Steve makes the Crocodile Environmental Park, previously a separate attraction open only for crocodile shows, part of the main zoo. The change, designed to better showcase the crocs, requires months of renovation and restructuring.

2000: Steve and Terri buy an additional 173 acres (70 hectares) with plans to eventually expand the zoo, which received approximately 200,000 people this year.

2001: Approximately 350,000 people visit the zoo.

2002: Approximately 600,000 people visit the zoo, beating out the previously reigning Dreamworld and Sea World to win the Queensland Tourism Industry Council's major award for best major tourist attraction.

2003: The Irwins unveil the Crocoseum, a massive arena designed for the zoo's wildly popular crocodile shows and major events, live on Animal Planet.

March 2008: Bob Irwin resigns from Australia Zoo. Terri denies plans to sell it, and announces plans to expand the zoo from 69 acres (28 hectares) to over 988 acres (400 hectares).

2010: Australia Zoo, which houses more than 1,000 animals of dozens of species, and employs more than 600 staff members, celebrates its fortieth anniversary (from the year of land purchase) with special events all year long.

Queensland National Parks and Wildlife Service was well aware of Bob Irwin's expertise in herpetology, particularly in the areas of safely capturing crocodiles and venomous snakes. The government often commissioned him to capture a particular species for conservation and study, and he'd bring his wide-eyed son along.

"WHAT'S THIS KID GOT?"

Of course, Steve wasn't allowed to go off and catch just anything on his own. Unfortunately for his dad's nerves, this didn't necessarily matter to the little boy. Perhaps the best example of Steve's unbridled curiosity is the story of a brown snake—a highly venomous species—he encountered at age seven, when the family still lived in Victoria. Bob and Steve were on a snake hunt in the bush when Steve noticed the slithering brown creature at his sandaled feet, literally flicking at one of them with its tongue. Bob had educated Steve well on identification of venomous snakes, and the boy knew he should never touch or bother one. Still, the pride his father would surely feel if he actually caught one, Steve thought, would outweigh any fury. He put his exposed foot right down firmly on the snake and excitedly called for his dad. Bob came running, took one look at the seething animal, and knocked his son out of the way. Bob was furious, all right, and Steve was crushed. Even so, the elder Irwin apparently couldn't hide a certain feeling of amazement at his offspring. "The snake was at my leg, poised, but wasn't biting," Steve said in the 2007 interview with Larry King. "And when he saw that, he thought to himself, what's this kid got?"

Knowing the answer full well, Bob became increasingly devoted to the nurture of Steve's instincts and enthusiasm. Within two years, he decided it was time to let Steve catch more than little things that slithered, crept, and crawled. It was time for his son to take the lead on a crocodile capture. Steve had helped out on crocodile projects many times before. His job was to hold the spotlight for his dad, then help hold down the small thrashing crocodile after Bob had caught it and heaved it into the boat. One day when Steve was nine, at his dad's request, he found himself sitting at the front of the boat—meaning that he'd be the one to actually jump the crocodile. Bob gave the word, and the next thing Steve knew, he was thrashing around in the river, holding on to a large freshwater crocodile with every muscle he had. The animal was 2 to 3 feet (0.6 to 0.9 m) longer than the Irwins had estimated from their limited, spotlit view into the murky water. "I remember seeing flashes of Dad's spotlight and I'm under the water, and I'm running out of air thinking *I am going to drown*, but there's no way that I was letting go of that croc, you know?" Steve told *Reader's Digest* magazine. "You can imagine how proud I was to be given that opportunity, so I'm just hanging on for grim death and getting thrashed around and around." Bob dragged the two of them into the boat just as Steve wondered if he could hold his breath any longer. Panting, Steve looked up at his dad's face and saw a distinct mix of worry and pride—the latter more apparent. It was, Steve told the magazine, "one of my greatest, if not my greatest childhood memory, [because] all I wanted to be was my dad."

"ONE WITH THE RIVER"

Over the next few years, the Beerwah Reptile Park held its own as a unique natural learning center. The Irwins put every penny of the modest but steady income the park earned right back into the facility's upkeep and growth. Meanwhile, Steve divided his time mainly among animal adventures, cricket and rugby matches, and studies at Caloundra High School, from which he graduated in 1979. By that time, it had become clear that the little park was now the most popular wildlife attraction in the state. Further, calling it simply a "reptile park" no longer suited the place because reptiles were no longer the only featured animals. It was time for a change—or two. In 1980, the Beerwah Reptile Park became the Queensland Reptile and Fauna Park (*fauna* refers to native animals), and with the Irwins' purchase of 4 acres (1.6 hectares) of adjoining property, it grew to twice its original size.

HOW TO CATCH A CROC

If you've ever tried to catch an animal, from a butterfly to your escaped dog, you know it can be a challenge. So, how does someone manage to catch a giant, wild reptile with jaws that can crush bones? The short answer would be: *very carefully*.

Gone are the days when the primary way to capture a crocodile was simply to "jump it" as it swam, as Steve did that first glorious time at age nine. Since then, specially designed traps have become the key to a successful crocodile catch, and setting them up is a project in itself. As Steve explained on the official Crocodile Hunter Web site, there are three distinct types of traps used today, and each has a distinct method of use. What follows is a brief look at each.

SOFT MESH TRAPS

The Irwins developed this original trapping technique, the only one Steve used until the 1990s. A mesh trap is usually set up on a sloping bank, secured along the sides with sticks driven into the mud, and kept in place with a rope secured by a steel ring to a sturdy tree. The trapping mechanism is a drawstring, created by weaving the rope through the mesh at the opening of the trap, which quickly pulls closed when the trap is triggered. The trigger involves suspending several weighted bags (filled with sand or dirt) attached to a piece of bait, such as a piece of feral pig (wild boar). The trapper decides how high and wide to make the trap, based on an estimate

Steve and Bob continued to team up on rescues and relocations of creatures large and small, but crocodiles dominated their efforts. In fact, these largest of reptiles were a primary motivation for expanding the park. An increasing number of "problem" saltwater crocodiles—those that had begun to venture into human-inhabited territory—were being killed as a way to take care of the problem.

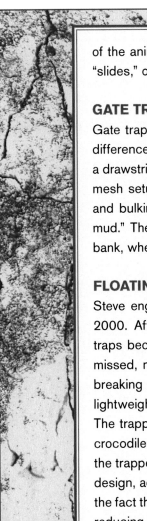

of the animal's size, which he or she can determine by looking for "slides," or crocodile tracks in the mud.

GATE TRAPS

Gate traps are a variation of the classic soft mesh trap. The main difference is that this trap uses a metal gate instead of weights and a drawstring. Although setup takes only about half the time that soft mesh setup takes, Steve noted, "The downside is the clumsiness and bulkiness of the gate in the boat and through the mangrove mud." The best place for a gate trap is a solid, hard-packed river bank, where there is no chance of the gate sinking.

FLOATING TRAPS

Steve engineered his first model of this innovative trap design in 2000. After some modification over the next few years, floating traps became "unbelievably successful," he wrote. "They've never missed, never failed and constantly [amaze] us with their record breaking success." As their name implies, these traps, made of lightweight aluminum and stainless steel, simply float on the water. The trapper uses a boat to tow the trap to a desired location, and crocodiles literally swim right in to get the bait. A gate closes, and the trapper's got a crocodile. There are many benefits to this newer design, according to Steve, including no need for land access and the fact that the crocodile stays submerged even when caught, thus reducing its stress.

Bob knew that there was a better way. From his outrage eventually sprang the Crocodile Environmental Park, a haven he and Steve built especially for these threatened animals.

In the late 1980s, when the Queensland Government's East Coast Crocodile Management program asked Steve to head north to hunt and capture wayward crocodiles, it was as if his life were

Bob Irwin puts the finishing touches on a wooden crocodile carved out of a tree at the Queensland Reptile and Fauna Park in March 1989.

unfolding neatly before him. He grabbed the chance, along with a mesh net, an aluminum dinghy, and his trusted dog Chilli, and set off for the crocodile-infested rivers of North Queensland. By Steve's own account, the months-long venture was no holiday. Trap-setting alone could be a painful ordeal. As if dragging a 264-pound (120-kilogram) bag (filled with sand or dirt, to serve as an anchor) uphill and into his dinghy wasn't hard enough in itself, Steve had to do it "while 5,000 green ants were biting on my eyeballs," he told *The Adelaide Advertiser.*

There was one particular crocodile the Queensland Government hoped Steve would be able to, literally, get his hands on. It was a huge, elusive black saltie that locals reported had been lurking in Cape York for years. So determined was Steve to return home with the animal that he "became one with the river," Terri wrote in *Steve & Me*. "He disregarded the mangrove mud that covered him until he was camouflaged as he sat silently in wait." It took months, but it eventually happened—one night the giant reptile became entangled in the mesh trap. Steve managed to get the crocodile into his dinghy, but getting the boat ashore required a little help. It was this predicament that allowed Steve to make the acquaintance of some nearby farmers and for those farmers to finally meet the legendary "black ghost." He was able to show the locals that Acco, as the crocodile was soon named, wasn't something to be wiped out and forgotten. Acco, like every one of his fellow modern-day dinosaurs, was something truly amazing.

The Crocodile Hunter

After talking to him and finding out that he absolutely lives for his conservation work, I was really attracted to those ethics and that really drew me in. . . . I think I fell in love with his spirit before noticing those great shorts.

—Terri Irwin

By the time the 1990s rolled around, Steve Irwin arguably had been a crocodile hunter for most of his life. It was just that only a handful of people really knew it. Within a few short years, however, that would change dramatically—and nearly overnight.

"THIS SHEILA WALKS INTO THE ZOO . . ."

Home again after his series of solo exploits in the Australian bush, Steve was ready to dive back into the family business. A highlight of his full-time work at the Queensland Reptile and Fauna Park was his role as crocodile trainer. Steve's innate skill and comfort level,

Terri Raines holds a 10-week-old male cougar club in Eugene, Oregon in 1991, the same year she met Steve Irwin.

his charisma, and his obvious passion made his live crocodile demonstrations a popular program. Most spectators were continental, but once in a while, an American might happen by. On an October day in 1991, one did—and so began a love story.

Steve and Agro, a trusty 13-foot (4-meter) saltie, were showing a small crowd of curious spectators just how smart, interesting, and surprisingly loving Steve's favorite order of animals could be. He explained that male saltwater crocodiles are territorial, as he carefully allowed Agro to lunge from the water and grab a piece of meat from his hand. He talked about the maternal instincts of the females. He said crocodiles show affection toward each other and actually have romantic relationships of sorts. All the while, according to a certain awestruck young woman who watched him that day, Steve's sole intention was clear: He wanted people to get to know and love crocodiles. "Instead of talking about his accomplishments, he was talking about what passionate lovers and beautiful mothers crocodiles are," Terri Irwin said in a live chat with MSN.com in 2001. "I was so impressed . . . . It was love at first sight." In numerous interviews, Steve echoed that last part.

TERRI RAINES, COUGAR CATCHER

Although Steve introduced Terri to countless types of animals, there is at least one species about which Terri surely did the educating. Long before she became the Crocodile Hunter's wife (or even made his acquaintance), Terri was already a wildlife warrior herself. She had made the rescue and rehabilitation of various mammals, particularly cougars, her life's work.

Like Steve's, Terri's dad had a soft spot for animals and would often bring injured ones back to the family's home in Eugene, Oregon. His successful trucking company had him frequenting highways, where he'd find creatures in need of help. Terri and one particular creature, a young cougar, took to one another so naturally that Terri adopted the cub as her own. Caring for Malina, as Terri named her, and for so many other animals inspired Terri to open her own wildlife rehabilitation center in 1986. There, she nurtured and re-educated predatory mammals (ones who prey on other animals)

Of course, for Steve, Terri herself was a sight indeed, especially after the life from which he'd just returned. "It's amazing how things happen," Steve told Larry King in 2004. "This sheila [Australian slang for an attractive girl] walks into the zoo. I've been up in North Queensland catching crocs for months on end, haven't seen a girl for a long time . . . . And I look into the crowd, and I'm, like, 'You're kidding.' This beautiful woman is, like, staring at me. . . . The crowd left, and she stayed." Unfortunately, she couldn't stay for long. Terri, then 27 and a cougar rehabilitator, was on a limited visit from her native Oregon to try to find homes for rescued American cougars. She soon left the country, but never, from that first day, Steve Irwin's life. After a whirlwind international courtship, the two married in her hometown of

for ultimate release back into their natural habitats. The roughly 300 creatures in her care each year ranged from raccoons and opossoms to bears and, of course, cougars. She aptly named the facility Cougar Country.

The words *puma*, *panther*, *mountain lion*, and *cougar* actually all describe the same species, for which *cougar* is the most general term. Cougars, the United States' largest cat, have a wide range of habitat, which runs from northwestern Canada down to the southern Andes Mountains in South America. In the United States, they live almost exclusively in the west, such as in Terri Irwin's native Oregon. In regions east of the Mississippi, they have become nearly extinct.

Between Terri's and Steve's expertise, it's no wonder the two quickly became the power couple of wildlife conservation. "When I came to Australia and met Steve," Terri told Australian talk show host Andrew Denton, "[it was like] reptile man meets mammal woman, and it was fantastic."

Eugene on June 4, 1992. Four hundred people watched as this next-generation pair of animal lovers said, "I do."

HONEYMOON . . . OR CROCUMENTARY?

The wedding champagne had barely lost its chill when Steve got the call. His friend John Stainton, a South Brisbane filmmaker with whom Steve had worked many times, had learned of a situation that seemed to beg Steve's involvement. Stainton had already received the green light from Australian TV producers to capture and air the crocodile hunter's daring rescues, and he couldn't let this particular opportunity simply slip away. Yes, it was only four days after the ceremony, and yes, the couple was packing in preparation for a romantic trip to the Pacific Northwest, but this was urgent—and he had to try.

As it turned out, the newlyweds agreed that a crocodile hunt on Cattle Creek, a river system up the coast from Brisbane, offered all the romance they needed. They quickly scrapped their original plans once John told them about a particular saltie whose life was in imminent danger. Steve's best mate and fellow herpetologist Wes Mannion accompanied the couple and John on the nontraditional honeymoon, where the group immediately got to work trying to locate the 14-foot-long (4.2-meter-long) creature.

They checked their strategically placed traps day after day, to no avail. They seemed to run into every creature—from lizards and venomous snakes to koalas and feral pigs—except the object of their search. Finally, they found it, but it was too late. Poachers (people who kill animals for profit) had shot the huge animal, which lay lifeless at the bottom of the river. "Steve had tears in his eyes," Terri recounted in *Steve & Me*. "This croc could have been 50 years old, with mates, a family, and a history of king of this river." To her new husband, every animal was an individual, a valuable being, a friend. His devastation at what he felt as a personal failure soon softened a bit as he and his crew managed to save a different crocodile before the trip was through. Best of all, for the first time ever, they had professional footage to prove it. Though the brave, elusive crocodile they tried so hard to rescue was lost, something would soon be born—an international sensation.

"BIGGER THAN BOTH OF US"

For Terri, the grand Oregon wedding had also served as a mass farewell since accepting Steve's proposal had meant agreeing to share his life in Australia. As John Stainton hunkered down to edit days' worth of footage into a documentary for broadcast, Terri and her new husband settled into life on the grounds of the Irwins' wildlife park. There was little time for rest, though. A project perhaps even more important than their documentary work required the couple's immediate attention. An unusual wedding gift from Steve's parents had awaited the newlyweds' return from Cattle Creek: a share in the park itself. Though Steve had begun managing the park the previous year, Bob and Lyn now gave their son and daughter-in-law half ownership.

Steve and Terri eagerly began making plans for the place, which they immediately renamed Australia Zoo. They wanted to expand and add new programs. They wanted to gain visibility and attract more visitors. They were determined to do whatever it took to save and protect wildlife. "When I met Steve," Terri recounted to Queensland's *Sunshine Coast Daily* in 2007, "there was something about him that made me feel like, 'Whoa, something is at work here that's bigger than both of us,' and that [had] been part of our lives, our work and our marriage ever since."

That something materialized, in the early years, in the form of a bigger and better wildlife park. From more attractive, inviting grounds to larger and more visible crocodile enclosures, Australia Zoo saw improvements every day. With little money to support their vision, Steve did much of the work himself, including planting trees, milling timber, and operating and repairing backhoes. Meanwhile, Terri, whose own work history involved mainly mammals, made

Steve Irwin and wife Terri have fun with Jonathon the Green Iguana at Australia Zoo in 1993, the year after they married.

efforts to become better acquainted with the zoo's scalier residents. Steve helped by encouraging her to spend time with Rosie, a favorite boa constrictor. With Steve's encouragement, Terri's nervousness quickly gave way to complete comfort. Soon, the gentle creature began to hang around Terri constantly—and literally. Rosie would rest comfortably around her new human buddy's shoulders as Terri went about her daily chores.

Both generations of Irwins, along with just three full-time staffers and one part-timer, did the best they could to maintain, improve, and market the zoo on a very limited budget. Like many in the early 1990s, they didn't have a personal computer with email, let alone a fax machine, to help. Within a couple of years, though, things would change. More help than the family could have imagined was on its way.

STARRING STEVO

Up to this point, the only opportunity most people had to see Steve Irwin in action required a visit to his zoo. Then, one evening, Aussies everywhere got the chance to virtually accompany him into the wild without having to travel at all. When the airing of John Stainton's Cattle Creek documentary on Australia's Channel 10 "caused a minor stir" of excitement, according to Terri in *Steve & Me,* the filmmaker and his budding stars jumped right in to give audiences more. Additional episodes of what had, by now, been titled *Crocodile Hunter,* soon followed the premiere. The show enjoyed instant success in major Australian cities, including Sydney, Melbourne, and especially Brisbane.

It certainly wasn't the first TV show in history to offer up-close encounters with wild animals. Still, it was like nothing viewers had seen. It focused on crocodile and other wildlife rescues, and the camera followed the host into unknown, potentially dangerous situations. Most significantly, though, the show featured someone whose mesmerizing talent lay in simply being himself. "Years ago, I started seeing things about [myself] in [the show] that I didn't like, and I was starting to change," Steve told the *Sydney Morning Herald* in 2002, years into the program's wildly popular run. "[John] said if we were gonna [sic] prosper and do this for the rest of our lives, I had to stay the same as I was the first day we met . . . 'Cause, deadset, the secret of our success is just havin' raw Stevo.'"

For the Irwins, the best part of that success was arguably the instant business boom it created for the zoo. Within months of *Crocodile Hunter's* debut, a day's total receipts had increased nearly sevenfold. Two passionate projects that had begun decades apart had joined forces, both in pursuit of the one common goal that would never change. "Every cent we earn goes back into conservation," Steve is widely quoted as having said at the height of success: "Every single cent."

DISCOVERED

If the Irwins thought continental success was nice, they hadn't seen anything yet. In the second half of the 1990s, *Crocodile Hunter* fever began to spread overseas, particularly to the United States. Once the right people caught a glimpse of this program that had become a near phenomenon in its native land, things started to happen fast.

By Terri's account, the first right person was Peter Jennings, host of ABC's *World News Tonight.* He had seen one of the documentaries and decided to feature Steve in a segment called "Person of the Week." For the first time, average Americans were able to meet this interesting Aussie in all of his engaging passion. Although nothing immediately or directly came of the Jennings honor, Terri, being American herself, knew it was a bit of publicity that couldn't be ignored. The Irwins had touched down, if only with a little toe, in the media capital of the world.

Within a couple of years, Terri found herself digging through a forgotten wardrobe of "power suits" from her pre-Australian life. It had been years since she'd had to wear one, but she felt her usual khakis wouldn't exactly be appropriate for the business meeting of a lifetime. Steve Irwin and *Crocodile Hunter* had made the radar

Steve Irwin, shown playfully interacting with a crocodile at his zoo in 1996, was known for his fearlessness with wild animals.

of cable-TV network Discovery Channel, and Terri, the marketing force behind the show, was on her way to the station's executive offices in Bethesda, Maryland. The opportunity to walk through those doors was a nature documenter's dream.

The executives' initial reaction to the show and Terri's pitch, however, wasn't exactly dreamlike. Ironically, the aspect that nagged them was the one that was the show's ultimate success factor: raw Stevo everywhere. It was something the world of wildlife programming simply wasn't used to because documentaries were traditionally "80 percent wildlife, 20 percent host," Terri wrote in *Steve & Me*. Still, the channel was intrigued, and the timing happened to be perfect: Discovery Channel had recently launched a

(*continues on page 42*)

CROCODILE FARMS: CONSERVATION OR CRUELTY?

The Australia Zoo is home to dozens of crocodiles and their American cousins, alligators. Zoos, however, are not the only facilities that keep crocodiles on their premises. Throughout coastal Australia, Africa, and other areas, there are places known as crocodile farms, where the animals are bred and prepared to make certain people a lot of money.

Crocodiles are a multimillion-dollar industry, mainly for their skins, which can be used to make high-end clothing and accessories. In some regions, people also eat their meat. Needless to say, many people oppose the killing of crocodiles, especially for profit. However, on some of these farms, the animals' living conditions alone are enough to incite outrage in naturalists. In *Steve & Me,* Terri describes a brief visit to a northern Queensland crocodile farm a few years into her marriage. Steve had taken her so that she could see for herself what was happening. There, the couple observed frightened, aggressive animals living in cramped conditions, many with serious injuries or terrible birth defects. Young crocodiles were kept in dark boxes, opened only for seconds at a time for feeding. Because the practice of crocodile farming is perfectly legal in Australia, there was nothing they could do.

Crocodile farmers fiercely defend their industry, many calling it a brand of conservation. "I'm a crocodile conservationist and farmer and I believe firmly that to protect the croc you have to make money from it," John Lever, owner of the Koorana Salt Water Crocodile Farm in central Queensland, told *The Sunday Mail* in 2007. "If you commercialize the crocodiles, the ones resident on people's properties, for example, they stop being these dreadful creatures that steal their sheep and become very valuable to them." At the time of the article, Queensland was considering a change in its saltie management plan, which would allow crocodile farmers to legally harvest crocodile eggs from the wild. Supporters call this conservation angle sustainable use; the Crocodile Hunter called it a crock. "Since when has killing animals saved a species?" Steve wrote on the Crocodile Hunter Web site. "The farming, killing, skinning and eating of native animals is a rife and evil industry, which operates under the cloak of science and lies." He had also spoken out against alligator farms, which exist mainly in the southern United States.

Some crocodile farms exist for the purpose of studying the animals and increasing their numbers. These farms are also known as crocodile banks or rehabilitation projects, and they may be open to the public. As Steve explained to Terri during their eye-opening visit, though, any crocodile farm "is an easy place to access crocodiles in great numbers"—indicating that researchers may simply come to for-profit crocodile farms to observe behavior. Steve spent his career urging people not to buy crocodile or alligator products. "If we can destroy the market," he wrote on his site, "we'll destroy the industry."

Juvenile saltwater crocodiles at a farm in Queensland, Australia, gather together in a small space. Critics of the croc farms call such living spaces inhumane.

(*continued from page 39*)

spinoff station called Animal Planet, and it was there that the parent company felt *Crocodile Hunter* just might find a suitable home. Animal Planet creator Clark Bunting "thought both Steve and the show were a nice complement to the Animal Planet brand," said an unnamed Discovery Channel executive, according to a 2006 article in *The Age*. "[Bunting] explored it, loved it and ultimately greenlit it for the network." With that, the exploring had only begun.

UNCHARTED TERRITORY

It was 1997, and Steve Irwin and his wife were now official faces in the world of American media. Shortly after the Animal Planet deal, came a *Dateline NBC* TV segment, where the host and crew of the popular news show accompanied the couple into the Australian bush. Steve had his first guest spot on *The Tonight Show* with Jay Leno, at the time the highest-rated U.S. talk show. His blend of expertise and quirky wit would later have Leno asking him back more than once. When Steve was later nominated for a CableACE award as host of the documentary *Ten Deadliest Snakes in the World,* he and Terri were whisked to Los Angeles for a black-tie affair (where Steve wore khakis). Life had changed—and it wasn't done yet.

Steve and Terri hadn't been back in Australia for long when Terri learned she was pregnant. The mom- and dad-to-be could not have been more thrilled with the news. Steve had recently told Terri that not only did he want to have children but also that he felt that they had to. Otherwise, he told her, their life's mission to rescue wildlife would itself become endangered. Terri was excited by the prospect of having a family with Steve, and now that idea was becoming a reality.

Fortunately, expecting a baby didn't mean Terri had to stop doing what she loved or even to slow down too much. "I was very lucky to be surrounded by doctors with common sense," Terri said in the

2001 MSN.com chat. "When I became pregnant my doctor said I can do everything I was currently doing, but don't take on any more. In the first trimester, I just had to deal with not letting myself get overheated."

Relieved by the medical go-ahead, Terri and Steve continued their regular commitment to both their zoo and their filming. One of their scheduled trips while waiting for baby turned out to be a particularly heartbreaking one. The couple and crew headed to a remote area on the island of Tasmania, off the southern coast of Australia, where they were met with a devastating situation. Dozens of sperm whales, including males, females (some pregnant), and calves, were stranded on the shore. Because the seas were very rough during Tasmanian summers, it was not possible to do anything for the whales but hold, talk to, and try to comfort them. Whale strandings (or "beached whales") are something of a cruel mystery to scientists, but some theories relate to the keen communication between the animals. "One animal gets into strife and the others come in to help it, and when they get in strife, more animals come in, and it sort of pyramids in and then you end up with a lot of animals on a beach," Ronny Ling, President of the whale rescue group ORRCA, told Australia's *G-Online*. Tasmania is Australia's most common region for strandings of this type, which experts say is likely due to conditions in the narrow channel between the island and the mainland. Unfortunately, rescues are difficult and often impossible. On this summer day in 1998, Terri, Steve, and their assistants gave all they could to the suffering animals. Terri wondered if their unborn child, whom she and Steve had nicknamed "Igor" (both were certain a boy was on the way), was somehow beginning his education through this sad but real experience.

Shortly after the Tasmania trip, Terri's doctor finally said it was time to take it easy, and Terri worked at the zoo while Steve continued to do field work. As it turned out, however, Terri's final month of pregnancy was really only days—ready or not, Baby Igor was coming a bit earlier than planned. Of course, both parents were met with a surprise when it wasn't little Igor at all, but a baby daughter, who arrived on July 24, 1998. "To hear Steve tell the story, it was like he gave birth," Terri told Larry King in 2007, speaking of her husband's hands-on role in their first child's delivery. "He's like, 'and then I got her out and it was great.' And I kept going, 'you know, I was there, too.'"

Years before, when Steve had announced that he and Terri had to have a child, Terri had played devil's advocate. She made the point that their child could end up becoming a shoe salesman in Malaysia. "Come off the grass," Steve had replied. "Any kid of ours is going to be a wildlife warrior." Time would quickly tell.

A Croc Catcher is Born

Now, she's six. And anyone who meets her finds her [to be] the most well-rounded, beautiful, and endearing child that anyone's ever met . . . She's a wildlife warrior and she's incredible.
—Steve Irwin

There had been little question that if Terri had a girl, the baby would be named after Steve's favorite female crocodile, Bindi, which is an Australian aboriginal word meaning "young girl." It then made perfect sense to honor Steve's beloved dog, Sui (his first girlfriend, he and Terri would joke), with their daughter's middle name. Now, a few weeks early but "all pink and perfect," Bindi Sue Irwin had arrived.

KHAKI-CLAD BUNDLE OF JOY

Having just helped deliver his daughter, new dad Steve gingerly handed her to Mom. Terri got only a few glorious seconds with little Bindi, though, before Steve suddenly took her back. There

Three-year-old Bindi Irwin gets into the family business, as she models an outfit from the children's fashion line named after her, Bindi Wear.

was simply too much joy for one hospital room to contain. Steve had to share this tiny new blessing with the entire maternity ward, and Mom understood. Soon enough, however, it was just the family of three again. Bindi's tiny eyes gazed at Steve, and he gazed back, "tears rolling down his cheeks," Terri wrote in *Steve & Me*. The family felt happy, safe, and complete.

From the get-go, Bindi's life was one big safari adventure. She hadn't been home a week before the Irwins packed up for their very first multilocation film shoot as a new family. After a quick stop in Queensland's subtropics to film the region's beautiful sea turtles, it was off to Mom's homeland—the United States. Assistants were on hand to stay with Bindi back at the car while Terri would quickly do her part on camera. Even on that first trip, however, newborn Bindi did get to see some harmless critters up close.

Bindi was drawn to her dad from the time that she arrived in this world. In the 2007 interview with Terri and Bindi, talk show host Larry King asked if Bindi was a daddy's girl. Terri didn't have to think for a second about the answer. "I can remember one time when Bindi said to me, 'Mom, I don't want to hurt your feelings, but I think I should tell you that I think I love daddy more,'" she told King. "I said, 'That's OK. It's great.'" It was back in those first weeks and even days of Bindi's life that the special bond began. According to Terri, Steve could both calm his infant daughter and make her more alert, and she would react when he'd simply walk past her room. Settled in back at home after the U.S. jaunt, Steve immediately began to introduce his daughter to her unique new world. He'd carry her all around the zoo to meet the rest of her "family"—the animals—and even do crocodile demonstrations while holding her. One photo shows Bindi dressed in what was quite possibly the tiniest ever Australia Zoo staff T-shirt, an official sign that this little girl was right where she belonged.

NURTURED IN NATURE

As Bindi grew, so did her exposure to the great outdoors. By the time she reached preschool age, her involvement in the family business

By the time she was 4 years old, Bindi Irwin had been on 302 flights across Australia and internationally—mostly due to her parents' work with animals. In this March 2003 image, she poses with her passport.

had gone from staying behind in the car to helping the team wrangle crocodiles. She enjoyed a life of travel and the wonderment of the animal world. If she wasn't jetting off to a distant jungle with her parents, she was playing in her own backyard, which just happened to be an internationally renowned zoo.

Depending on the location and nature of the film shoot, Mom and Bindi would sometimes tend to the home front while Dad went off on location. As often as possible, however, filming was a family affair. One early video on the Discovery Kids Web site shows a film crew member, Grant, playing with a khaki-clad baby Bindi in a red-sanded desert setting. "You want to face the camera like Daddy does?" Grant asks, holding up the one-year-old girl. "Talk about the rock behind you. Off you go." Bindi decides to reach out and smack the camera—and then a chuckling Grant—instead.

Young Bindi not only adored but seemed to truly appreciate animals, and even shared her dad's famous ability to communicate with them. Terri told ABC's *Good Morning America* that when Bindi was 18 months old, she would lull her pet python to sleep by singing to it. In fact, there was seemingly no creature that couldn't find a place in the little girl's heart. On the Crocodile Hunter Web site, Terri describes one of her favorite stories from Bindi's animal-filled toddlerhood. "Bindi proudly held up a fully engorged leech that had fallen out of Steve's sock," she writes. "I quickly grabbed it to toss it out, when the tears started to flow. So, as a family, we went into the backyard and released that plump little leech. Bindi was content that we had done the right thing. We could all learn a lesson from such open, honest, innocent love." No one could argue it now. Steve had his little wildlife warrior.

"SHE LOVED ME ALL MY LIFE"

For a year and a half after Bindi's birth, Steve and Terri reveled in their many blessings. Their zoo was flourishing. *Crocodile Hunter* was an international hit. Steve had even started work on a spinoff, *Croc Files*, which would air on Discovery Channel's subsidiary, Discovery Kids. Above all that, of course, was the beautiful daughter

HAZARDS OF BEING
THE CROCODILE HUNTER

It certainly didn't seem like the safest line of work. Every day, if Steve Irwin wasn't wrangling a razor-toothed reptile up to 10 times his weight, he might have been trying to capture one of the world's deadliest snakes. Some people might conclude that he was a little out of his mind, a suspicion which was, apparently, just fine with him. "I think it's good that people think I'm a little crazy or a little nuts," he told the *Worcester Telegram & Gazette* on the opening day of his 2002 film *The Crocodile Hunter.* "Because one thing is for sure: I don't want anyone doing what I do."

As the article noted, the constant peril was "all in a day's work" for the crocodile hunter. Rather than downplay the danger, Steve would emphasize that he had been living among animals since birth and had "a gift" for dealing with them safely. Still, he didn't get out of every situation unscathed and had the battle scars to prove it. "Have I ever," was Steve's response when Larry King asked if he'd ever been injured by an animal. "This [finger] got snapped off. I'd been catching crocodiles in North Queensland putting [on] satellite

who had made them into a family. As a reporter once stated in a news feature about Steve, "the only thing that could ever keep him away from the animals he loves are the people he loves even more." Even during his childhood, on a homestead filled with wildlife, family had always come first—which made what happened next that much less bearable.

A year that had promised to be even better than the last began with unspeakable tragedy. In February 2000, Terri and Bindi were on a visit to Oregon when Terri received an early morning call. On

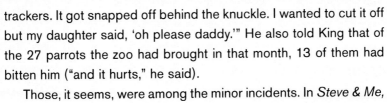

trackers. It got snapped off behind the knuckle. I wanted to cut it off but my daughter said, 'oh please daddy.'" He also told King that of the 27 parrots the zoo had brought in that month, 13 of them had bitten him ("and it hurts," he said).

Those, it seems, were among the minor incidents. In *Steve & Me,* Terri recounted a time when a resident crocodile grabbed Steve's thigh in her jaws during an enclosure transfer. Terri was horrified to see blood trickling down his leg and "a dozen tears in the fabric of his khaki shorts." In his usual style, Steve made no fuss at the time but did end up with some loss of sensation on that patch of flesh. Another time, a crocodile grabbed Steve's hand and actually "pulled me in the water to kill me," Steve told *Reader's Digest* (Australia). Fortunately, his gift came in handy once again, and he escaped.

According to Terri, it seemed there was never a week when Steve "didn't get a bite, blow, or injury of some kind," although he told interviewer Larry King that he did manage to avoid venomous snake bites. How and why he could do what he did, day in and day out, was something that surprised even Steve. "I don't understand it," he told the *Telegram Gazette.* "I'm living it. It just seems completely normal. I just can't explain it."

the other end, Steve, sobbing and "incoherent," managed to give her a devastating message: His mother, Lyn, had been killed in a car crash. Only in her mid-fifties, Lyn and her husband had been looking forward to a whole new adventure. They were about to move closer to their son and his family, closer to their precious granddaughter, who was only 18 months old. When she died, Lyn had been transporting a final few belongings to her new home.

The tragedy cut Steve to his core. Lyn was not only "his greatest inspiration" in the field of wildlife conservation, Terri wrote, but also a lifelong source of strength for her only son. Their connection had been notably close. "I loved my Mum more than anything in the world," Steve later wrote in a tribute to her on the Australia Zoo Web site. "She nurtured, protected, and loved me all my life." Steve's devastation ran so deep that, at first, it threatened everything for which he had worked. He lost interest in projects and talked of moving away from the zoo. Terri wrote in *Steve & Me* that "time appeared to slow down and then stop entirely." After a brief trip into the bush with only his dog Sui by his side, Steve poured his raw emotions into expansion of the zoo. With backhoe and bulldozer, he worked hard on the land with plans to create better access for visitors and even a new hospital for injured animals. It would be a long time before Steve returned to something close to his old self, and, according to Terri, he never quite recovered completely.

Later that year, to honor his mum's gift for nurturing sick, injured, and orphaned animals, Steve founded the Lyn Irwin Memorial Fund. All donations would go directly to Iron Bark Station, the family's wildlife rehabilitation facility. This gesture and all that her son did in the years that followed would undoubtedly have made Lyn proud—which may have been his very intention. "I miss you every minute of every day, and the pain of losing you tears my heart out," Steve wrote in his tribute. "But I'll stay strong; I promise you I'll stay strong—for it was you who taught me to be a 'wildlife warrior.'"

HELLO HOLLYWOOD

Meanwhile, life went on for Steve's public, who seemed more smitten by the day. *Croc Files,* which could be described as a sort of *Crocodile Hunter* for the younger generation, was nominated for a Daytime Emmy Award in the category of Outstanding Children's Series. His heart still heavy with grief, Steve attended the ceremonies with Terri in Los Angeles. Although *Bill Nye the Science Guy* took the prize, Steve and Terri knew the recognition accompanying the nomination was an honor. Within a year, Steve had agreed to a second *Crocodile Hunter* spinoff. This one would offer a day-to-day

Steve and Terri Irwin film a scene for *The Crocodile Hunter: Collision Course* in 2002. The film had no script, so all dialogue was made up on the spot by the actors.

look at the lives of the Irwins and their broader family, including members of their film crews and staff at their zoo. *Crocodile Hunter Diaries* premiered on Animal Planet in 2001. Because of the show's reality format, little Bindi got to play an important role in many episodes—her charming self.

As the Irwins became more involved with American media, people with more power began to notice. MGM Studios in Holly-wood recognized that Steve's charisma and popularity had become too big for the small screen alone. It was time to make a feature film. Shortly after the 2000 Emmy Awards, MGM Studios and the Irwins began talking about a fictional adventure movie based on *Crocodile Hunter.* John Stainton, the man responsible for inciting *Crocodile Hunter* fever to begin with, would write and direct it.

Negotiations would continue for nearly two years before a contract was signed. A central issue was Steve's insistence that no animal encounter be faked, much less computer-generated. To keep the conservation message genuine, he explained, he would need to handle all animals himself. This unconventional agreement would mean complications with insurance, and because of these complications, the project was temporarily stalled. After a short break, how-ever, Steve, John, producer Judi Bailey, and the crew decided to take a risk. Unwilling to either compromise their conservation beliefs or give up on the film, they went ahead and shot the necessary crocodile-wrangling footage on their own, in hopes this would put insurance concerns to rest. It worked, and the making of *Crocodile Hunter: Collision Course* was officially underway.

The combination of Hollywood's imagination and Steve's natural appeal made for some action-packed fun. In the story, a crocodile (played by Charlie, one of the Irwins' own) has swallowed a track-ing device from a satellite that has fallen to earth. Steve, in the title role, needs to save the crocodile from CIA agents determined to get their hands on the animal. The crocodile hunter, unaware of the true situation, takes the agents for poachers, which thickens the zany plot. "What audiences are likely to enjoy the most are the scenes of Mr. Irwin in the natural habitat of croc-infested Northern Queensland

WILDLIFE WARRIORS

On a list of expressions that a person might associate with Steve Irwin, "wildlife warrior" would be right up there with his signature "crikey!" Irwin coined the term *wildlife warrior* early in his career because it seemed a perfect way to describe someone whose mission in life was to save the earth's creatures. It's also the perfect name for one of the world's most prominent wildlife conservation groups because the original warrior himself is the reason it all began.

In 2002, Steve and Terri founded what is now Australia Zoo Wildlife Warriors Worldwide Ltd. (WWW) (originally called the Steve Irwin Conservation Foundation) as a way to join forces with others who shared their goals. Although WWW is an independent organization today, Australia Zoo remains its major sponsor, and Terri is one of its primary advisors and closest friends. According to its Web site, the group's objectives are as follows:

- to protect and enhance the natural environment;
- to provide information and education to the public and raise awareness of wildlife issues;
- to undertake biological research;
- to research, recommend, and act in the protection of threatened or endangered species; and
- to enter into cooperative arrangements with like-minded organizations.

To uphold its missions, the Queensland-based group is involved with multiple wildlife rescue and protection efforts at any given time. In Sumatra, they patrol lands looking for poachers who might be after tigers. In South Africa, they work to safely manage cheetahs whose habitats are threatened by development. In the

(continues)

(continued)

world's oceans, they track and tag whales in order to research their populations. For a wildlife warrior, the job is never done—and inspiration is never far from thought. "We will miss you, boss," the group's Web site (www.wildlifewarriors.org.au) reads, "but we promise to put our hearts and souls into it for conservation, just like you did—everyday."

doing what the title of the film says he does," wrote Richard Duckett in a Worcester, Massachusetts, *Telegram & Gazette* article, after an interview with Steve and Terri on the film's opening day in 2002. "Some sequences with snakes and spiders also got some shrieks out of young audience members at a recent screening of the film."

Even as the star of a major motion picture, Steve's priorities never wavered. His wife and daughter were with him on location, and for Steve, breaks meant opportunities for him and Bindi to check out the area's wildlife. "Between takes, sometimes there was an hour set up if we were relighting the scene, and we'd lose Steve," John Stainton said in an interview with About.com writer Rebecca Murray. "We'd have to send someone out looking for him. He and Bindi would be up in the bush and he'd have a snake showing it to Bindi." The adventures continued even when filming ended because it was then time for the family's multistop promotional tour. With her parents, Bindi got to see much of the United States and mingle with Hollywood stars. At the first stop, Las Vegas, the Irwins participated in a movie-theater exhibition called *Show West*. There, Bindi found a buddy in host Bruce Willis and got to bring a ball python on stage for the *Collision Course* presentation. Visits to a dozen more North American cities and three in Europe followed. While the barely four-year-old Bindi had fun, Terri expressed to writer Murray that she probably would have preferred to be playing with her beloved animals back home. After all, they were family, too.

In the midst of American movie madness—Steve also had a small part in the 2001 film *Dr. Dolittle 2*, starring Eddie Murphy—Australia's own media industry came calling. Now that Steve had both a hit children's show and a small child of his own, his next project seemed natural: collaboration with premiere Aussie kids' entertainers The Wiggles. The result was *Wiggly Safari*, a 2002 video that takes Wiggles Anthony Field, Murray Cook, Greg Page, and Jeff Fatt on a visit to the Australia Zoo. The entire Irwin family gets in on the song-and-dance action as they teach viewers about various species of wildlife. "That was a stack of fun," Steve said of the experience in an interview with *Reader's Digest* (Australia). "The Wiggles are great people. I was hoping to be the fifth Wiggle, you know, but they are not going to have me." The one who probably made out best in the deal was Bindi. After all, she got to flit like a butterfly with Dorothy the Dinosaur and flap like a cockatoo alongside Captain Feathersword himself. As any four-year-old child would attest, life doesn't get much better.

COMMITMENT TO WILDLIFE

Though the Irwins enjoyed this world of entertainment media, they certainly never got lost in it. On the contrary, Steve often expressed feeling out of his element in the Hollywood scene. In the *Reader's Digest* interview, he did give a "shout out" to a few celebrities—namely actors Matt Damon, Will Smith, Antonio Banderas, Melanie Griffith, and Chris Tucker—with whom he seemed to click. "We just joked and laughed and told stories and enjoyed each other's company and they are really nice people and made me feel at home," he said, describing a recent visit to Los Angeles. "I sure appreciated that because you know I feel very much like a fish out of water over there, and they just made me feel like I was at home and they were proud of what I was doing, my commitment to wildlife."

That commitment remained at the center of everything Steve did. In fact, to him, the biggest benefit of stardom was its allowing him to promote conservation in greater ways than ever before. In addition to the countless media outlets—from talk shows to magazines to his own multiple programs—through which he could now spread his message, there was the income. Dollar signs for Steve, though, did not translate into vacation homes or luxury cars. All he thought about were conservation projects that previously had seemed distant dreams. Throughout his career, some Australians criticized Steve for the stereotypical, over-the-top Aussie image they felt he conveyed to America and the world. Others, though, had a more accurate take. As Anna King Murdoch wrote in a 2003 article for *The Age,* "His wild showmanship is one of the smartest fronts in the country. It makes him masses of money, which allows him a deeply quiet passion: conserving as much of the flora and fauna of Australia—and increasingly the rest of the world—as he possibly can before he dies."

People who knew Steve well might take issue with the term *front,* since by all accounts, the "raw Stevo" audiences saw is exactly who he was. Murdoch's general message, however, was one that no one could rightly deny. Steve's earnings allowed him to start the Steve Irwin Conservation Foundation (later renamed Wildlife Warriors Worldwide), an organization dedicated to the protection of endangered and threatened wildlife, in 2002. To jump-start the effort, he bought thousands of acres of land in Australia, the United States, and other parts of the world because protecting animals begins with protecting their natural habitats. He was also able to make once-lofty ideas for the zoo, such as the building of a 5,000-seat Crocoseum, a reality. (Zoo proceeds, in turn, are channeled directly back into conservation efforts.) None of it would have been possible without that very basic—and very smart—first step: inviting people in. As he put it to *Scientific American* in 2001, "I'm trying my darnedest to get my show, our show, into every single country in the world. Because *it works.*"

Finding Strength
After Tragedy

*We eat, sleep, and live for conservation. That's all we're about,
that's what we're up to, that's our game. And we will die defend-
ing wildlife and wilderness areas. That's our passion.*

—Steve Irwin

For the Irwin family, the turn of the millennium had been a
whirlwind of joy and excitement, pain and loss. The next few
years would bring more of each—in measures no one ever would
have imagined.

A GROWING ZOO

It was no secret that Steve had passion, charisma, and an uncanny
way with wildlife. What people may not have realized was that he
was also something of an engineer. In 2002, he envisioned something that no one had ever imagined before. Inspired by Roman
coliseums, the magnificent arenas where gladiators of the earliest

59

centuries A.D. held public duels, Steve wanted to build such a venue for crocodile shows. (One avid Irwin fan blogged that Steve was specifically inspired by the film *Gladiator,* which starred fellow Aussie and Steve's good "mate," Russell Crowe.) Business at the zoo had sharply increased when Steve's TV shows started to air. That trend continued over the years, and with the release of his feature film, numbers of visitors had gone through the roof. It was getting harder to accommodate the crowds, who mainly came to see the animals who shared Steve's fame: the crocodiles.

Steve enthusiastically sketched out his idea for Terri. The imagined facility included crocodile ponds connected via canals to a

Australian actor Russell Crowe (*left*) and late night TV talk show host Jay Leno (*right*) joke with Steve Irwin during a taping of Leno's show on November 6, 2003.

large pool in the middle of the arena. Although his wife and friends couldn't help but express a little skepticism, Steve's determination was so fierce that they soon had to share it. Steve had a dream, and its name was the Crocoseum. Steve and crew got to work.

By June 2003, the Crocoseum was no longer a dream, but an actual colossal structure that would seat 5,500 people. Not only did Steve's crocodile canal idea work out as sketched, but also the facility was built complete with a museum, gift shops, and a food court beneath it. Something this huge warranted the grandest of grand openings. If Australia Zoo was the crocodile hunter's actual home, then Animal Planet was his virtual one. Together the two created the channel's "first-ever live event and the biggest day in Australia Zoo history," spectator Robin M. Bennefield wrote on the Animal Planet fansite. Bennefield described a "surreal" scene centered around the world's largest single-propeller helicopter as it attempted to safely relocate 800-pound (362.8-kilograms) Monty and his smaller zoo-mates Goldie and Occy to their new home on June 9, 2003. Dozens of zoo staff and TV crew assisted in the daunting operation, each sharply focused on his or her specific task despite the day's drizzly rain and shifting winds. In the end, the team succeeded, and audiences the world over were not disappointed. Wrote Bennefield of Steve: "At the moment, the Triple Croc Pond is his coliseum and instead of slaying beasts, he's saving crocs and the crowds erupt in cheers."

A GROWING FAMILY

Around this time, Australia Zoo wasn't all that was expanding in the Irwins' world. Terri's belly was, too. She and Steve were elated to find out they would be expecting their second child later that year. The couple hoped for a boy to round out their happy family, although Bindi dreamed of a baby sister. In the end, her parents' wish won out. Robert Clarence "Bob" Irwin, named after each of his grandfathers, joined the family on December 1, 2003, an early and wonderful Christmas present for the whole family. When her dad raced to her school to tell her the news, even five-year-old Bindi was thrilled. "He told me that the baby's been born, and I was like, 'aaaaah, the baby's born!'" Bindi recalled in a televised interview not long after the joyful event. "I was of course a big sister, and I was really excited." A little brother, it seemed, would be good after all.

Naturally, there were only two things Steve now wanted to do: share his world with his new son and share his new son with the world. Just as he'd done with Bindi, Steve took baby Bob everywhere throughout the zoo to meet staff and his vast animal family. When Bob was one month old, Steve and Terri invited a group of Tibetan nuns to come bless him and their animals, as they had done for Bindi at that age. Steve's relationship with Tibetan Buddhism had begun when a monk visited his father at the zoo decades before. The monk had called Steve a "yogi," which angered the eight-year-old boy. He learned later that the monk did not mean to liken him to the popular cartoon character Yogi Bear. A yogi is "a person with a higher realisation [sic], in his instance of wildlife and the ability to harness the fear of animals." The spiritual master had seen something in Steve before the young naturalist was even old enough to recognize it in himself.

The Irwins held a special ceremony in the Crocoseum and invited the press. A crocodile show followed the blessing, and as Steve had done with his infant daughter, Steve carried Bob to the demo area. He introduced Bob to visitors and pointed out the crocodiles to his son. It wasn't the first (and wouldn't be the last) time Steve had baby Bob around crocodiles, but it was the first time multiple cameras captured it. That, sadly and near instantly, made all the difference. By that evening, footage of Steve and baby Bob was all over the news. Steve primarily held the child under his arm while feeding crocodiles, but at one point, he briefly placed him down closer to the pond. Some media compared the incident to Michael Jackson's actions in 2002, when the pop star dangled his infant son over a balcony to pacify a throng of screaming fans in Berlin. Jackson had been crucified in the press. Now it was Steve who was under media attack.

Not only were the two cases like apples and oranges, Steve's supporters claimed, but also Steve had no experience with this kind

Steve Irwin holds his one-month-old son, Bob, as he feeds a crocodile during a presentation at his zoo in 2004. Video from the performance was picked up by Australian TV news stations and quickly made international news.

of "casual cruelty," as Terri called it—and had no idea what had hit him. "I wasn't just shocked, I was absolutely devastated," Steve told Larry King in 2004. "I was taken to the lowest point of my entire life." A standard, thorough investigation by child protective services turned up nothing. This, of course, was no surprise to the Irwins, who adamantly maintained that Bob was never in any danger. (Steve's subsequent apology on the *Today* show, he told King, was "for scaring people.") Steve said in several interviews that deceptive camera angles, which he called "stacked shots," likely also contributed to the public's misperception. The bottom line, Steve and Terri told Australian talk show host Andrew Denton, was simple: For the Irwins, early exposure to animals ("It's not like we were teaching Robert how to hand feed a crocodile," Terri pointed out) was a natural way of life—and Steve had the skills and experience to know what's safe. "I want to raise my children the same as my parents raised me," Steve said. "I think that's the secret to good parenting, is [to] use techniques that you know work."

The pain of the ordeal and the threats to Steve's career (sponsors, TV crew members, and Discovery Channel executives were wary) gradually seemed to fade. Although Steve and Terri would

At age two, Bob was already comfortable with wild animals. In this 2005 image, he poses with his father and sister and a 3-year-old alligator named Russ at Australia Zoo.

never forget the awful experience, their warrior spirits were stronger than anything else. The newly completed family of four had work to do.

JUNGLE GIRL

In the wake of the controversy, Steve continued to do what he did best, which was show the world its wildlife. He and John Stainton literally took their crew to the ends of the earth to shoot *Icebreaker,* a documentary on animals of Antarctica. It was an eye-opening experience even for the wildlife master himself. He was fascinated by the world of humpback whales, leopard seals, and penguins, and he wanted to show audiences how they live and play. Unfortunately for him, a now-alert media was watching. Steve was accused of breaking Antarctic regulations on human interaction with penguins. Reports claimed he was interfering with them in ways that, if founded, could result in jail time. Steve seemed to take this latest matter in stride, calling the Australian authorities' investigation "just a big storm in a tea cup," BBC News reported at the time. He was cleared of all charges.

Steve and his family were constantly thinking of what more they could do to inspire people. As the decade neared its midpoint, thoughts increasingly began to point toward a certain spunky young Aussie. Here was a girl who had recently donated her tooth-fairy money to a koala hospital and spent vacations catching lizards, so she clearly had the right interests. In addition, she now had more TV experience under her belt than many kids in the center of Hollywood and more animal expertise than perhaps any child on Earth. Though a cliché, it was true—kids were the future. Who better to get them excited about conservation than one of their own? The concept of *Bindi the Jungle Girl* was born.

John Stainton would produce the show, which would air on Discovery Kids, home of Steve's *Croc Files*. Although Bindi would host the show and be the main star, Steve would appear as well. In his usual fashion, Steve could not wait to spread the exciting news of this father-daughter venture. He announced the planned project on the Jay Leno show during his visit to Los Angeles for *G'Day USA: Australia Week,* an annual promotional event for Australian tourism,

"IF ANYTHING HAPPENS TO ME . . ."

Steve Irwin, by his own description, was a man in a hurry. For him, there was no better time than the present. An idea would hit, and he would be off and running. Maybe he was just efficient with his time—or maybe he somehow knew it was limited.

After her husband's death, Terri often spoke about Steve's feeling that he would not be around long. Convinced he would not live to see 40, Steve would seek assurance that she, their children, and the zoo would be well taken care of if anything happened to him. "He said it constantly. He said it publicly. We discussed it," Terri told interviewer Larry King in 2007. "But neither of us ever thought there would be a situation . . . with wildlife. . . . I would have expected it from a car accident, from, perhaps, political unrest from a remote area where he was filming . . . [but] not from an animal, ever, never."

Steve's thoughts about mortality seemed to increase after the death of his own mother. Although he always acknowledged the potentially deadly hazards of his job, the manner of Lyn Irwin's death scared him more. "Driving here this car came screaming up to the traffic lights, hit the brakes and nearly creamed us," Steve once told the Australian Associated Press. "My mum was killed in a car crash, so although I can get killed by wildlife, I do live in fear of fast cars."

Sixth sense or realistic attitude, Steve knew there was no time to waste. He had a job to do, and he was ready for whatever might come with it. "I put my *life* on the line to save animals," he said in a 2000 interview with *Scientific American.* "I have no fear of losing my life—if I have to save a koala or a crocodile or a kangaroo or a snake, mate, I will save it."

in January 2006. Now, in addition to shooting for his own documentaries while out in the wild, Steve and crew began to gather footage for *Jungle Girl* as well.

A perfect opportunity for the young host-in-training presented itself in July 2006. The whole family would travel to Cape York Peninsula for five weeks of crocodile research, and for the first time, Bindi would have a vested interest in what the TV crew captured. Although July meant the dead of winter in Queensland, it was nearly always mild and sunny there. The trip promised to be an enjoyable, productive, and adventurous one, and it was. Terri noted in *Steve & Me* how Bindi, who she'd always seen as "a wise being in a little person's body," took it upon herself to get very involved in the filming. She wanted to make sure that her desired conservation messages, in images and words, would come across. The highlight of the trip was, arguably, Bindi's getting to jump a crocodile for the first time. Once Steve had safely secured the female crocodile's jaws, it was the point person's—Bindi's—time to shine. She did her job right on cue, and the rest of the rescue team (including Robert at two and a half) immediately followed, throwing themselves on the creature's scaly body. People on the Irwins' Christmas card list enjoyed a snapshot of this once-in-a-lifetime moment later that year.

LOSS BEYOND WORDS

It had been a fantastic five weeks. It had been productive, as Steve and the team had trapped dozens of crocodiles. It had been educational, as Bindi and even little Robert had learned some tricks of the trade they would carry forever. Then, with the family's evenings spent sitting together on their boat, watching bats fly overhead in a peaceful and dusky sky, it had been a particularly special trip, too.

At the end of it, though, Dad and the other three Irwins had to part ways. Terri, Bindi, and Robert, along with Bindi's teacher Emma and her sister Kate (also a zoo employee), were scheduled to head to Tasmania after a brief stop back at the zoo. Terri was to help investigate a cancer epidemic among Tasmanian devils, a species in which Steve and Terri had long had a keen interest. Steve and the crew would stay in Cape York, where they would team up with oceanographer Philippe Cousteau, grandson of the legendary Jacques. They would shoot footage in the Great Barrier Reef for a collaborative documentary called *Ocean's Deadliest.* This break in family time wasn't to be as long as some, though, because Terri and

STINGRAY RAGE?

You've heard the expression "an eye for an eye." In the wake of Steve Irwin's death, it looked like some people had taken this idea to a new level. Reports surfaced that at least 10 stingrays had been found dead in Queensland waters one week after a stingray had killed Steve. It appeared that someone had killed them intentionally because in at least two cases, their tails had been cut off.

Was this revenge for what one of their own had done to the crocodile hunter? "At the moment, that is just speculation," Wayne Sumpton, a senior biologist in Queenland's fisheries department, told a reporter for the U.K. newspaper *The Independent* that week. "We do find dead stingrays with their tails cut off from time to time. People usually do it if they are worried about getting stung, or they just do it maliciously, but it is pretty rare." Also rare are instances of stingrays killing or seriously harming humans. These animals generally only use the jagged, poisonous barb (part of the tail) that killed Steve when threatened. They are actually known to swim relatively close to divers in the warm shallow waters they inhabit, and neither bothers the other. These facts are what made the events of September 4, 2006 seem that much more bizarre.

No real evidence ever arose that the stingray deaths were acts of vengeance, and the world will likely never know the truth. Steve's own Wildlife Warriors spoke out loudly against this type of cruelty, whether or not "stingray rage" (as the United Kingdom's

Steve would be done with their respective duties in less than two weeks. Everyone except Steve boarded a small plane destined for home. It was time for good-bye, but only for a while.

The first few days of the Tasmania trip were all they should have been. Terri worked with a wildlife park to plan care for, and

TimesOnline called it) related to Steve's death was behind it. "We are disgusted and disappointed that people would take this sort of action to hurt wildlife," said Michael Hornby, the group's executive director and a good friend of Steve's. "We just want to make it very clear that we will not accept and not stand for anyone who has taken a form of retribution. That's the last thing Steve would want."

Stingrays, like this one swimming at the Sydney Aquarium in Australia, have a barbed stinger on their tail, which is used for self-defense.

management of, the ailing Tasmanian devils. She and the kids took in sights and made some tourist stops. They couldn't reach the very busy Steve, but they received some word on his adventures through a zoo employee, via satellite. On the day they arrived at a resort in Cradle Mountain National Park, though, things were not as they should have been at all. The woman at the front desk handed Terri a note that said Frank, who was the husband of Steve's sister, Joy, had called. That wasn't an odd thing, but the woman's suggestion that Terri return the call in private was. Still, Terri wasn't too concerned with the call, until Frank said that Steve had had an accident. He explained that Steve had been pierced in the chest by a stingray's barb. There was no painless way to give his sister-in-law the worst of it, so Frank gently went on to say what Terri, by that point, knew in her heart: Steve had died.

The rest of Terri's group, which included Bindi, Robert, and their caregivers, had not even entered the building yet. "I'm looking out the window watching Emma with a dancing Bindi, you know, in the garden," Terri told Larry King in 2007. "And Robert was asleep in the car and Kate was with him. And that was my first concern, was . for my children." On September 4, 2006, phone in hand, Terri went from living a dream to having to face the worst kind of nightmare.

THE BEST FRIEND THEY EVER HAD

The shocking death of Steve Irwin was huge news worldwide. From Hollywood stars to Australia's Parliament, from wildlife activists to fans of his shows, people everywhere mourned. The original wildlife warrior, who had made an immeasurable impact on this world that animals and humans shared, was gone. It seemed unreal.

Although sadness and disbelief were the main reactions, questions and arguments inevitably surfaced as well. Some wanted to know how this possibly could have happened, whereas others thought something of this nature had been bound to happen. John Stainton, who actually caught the sudden incident on film, did note that Steve was much more of a pro on land than in the sea. "If ever

Flowers and tributes to Steve Irwin fill an entryway to Australia Zoo on September 5, 2006.

he was going to go, we always said it was going to be the ocean," Stainton told the media. "On land he was agile, quick-thinking [and] quick-moving, and the ocean puts another element there that you have no control over." Still, there was no evidence that Steve had done anything to intimidate or threaten the stingray, and deaths from stingray barbs are extremely rare. (Incidentally, Steve and crew were gathering low-key footage for *Jungle Girl,* not filming for *Ocean's Deadliest,* when the tragedy happened.) The only theory even experts could surmise was that the animal may have felt trapped between Steve and Stainton. Terri had a simpler explanation. "It was a total fluke," she told Larry King a year after Steve's death. "I think I'd have to compare it to someone who was like a timber feller and he goes on a picnic and a limb falls on his head from a tree. It was that ironic."

Of course, the existence of actual footage of the incident was of major interest to many. There were the officials to whom the videotape was an invaluable investigative tool. There were also plenty of people driven by simple morbid curiosity. Clips that claimed to be "Steve Irwin's death video" sprang up almost immediately on YouTube and other sites. The odds that any were genuine, it seems, are next to zero. "When [the footage] is finally released [by authorities], it will never see the light of day," John Stainton told interviewer Larry King days after the incident. "Ever. Ever. I actually saw it, but I don't want to see it again." Terri, who had declined to ever view the tape herself, told King in a later interview that the footage had been destroyed.

Though the family would have to deal with the media frenzy that they would meet at every turn in the days that followed, those meetings were the least of their concerns. Two young children had lost their loving dad, and a woman, her soul mate. Even as she grappled with his death and where to go from here, Terri found that Steve, in a way, was still a source of support. "At six feet [183 centimeters] tall and two hundred [910 kilograms] pounds, he was a force to be reckoned with," Terri wrote in *Steve & Me.* "But he always told me there were different kinds of strength. Steve said he could count on me to be strong when times were hard."

Having declined Australian Prime Minister John Howard's offer of a state funeral, the family had a small private funeral at Australia Zoo five days after Steve's death. On September 20, they held

Bindi reads a speech about her father at a memorial service for him at Australia Zoo on September 20, 2006.

a public memorial service at the venue Steve surely would have chosen himself: his own Crocoseum. Thousands showed up for the moving event, where one seat, next to Terri, Bindi, and Robert, was symbolically left unoccupied. Prime Minister Howard, who had been asked to give opening comments, told the family that "there are 20 million pairs of Australian arms reaching out to embrace you this morning, to express our love and respect for what your beloved Steve . . . gave to Australia, gave to the creatures of this earth, and gave to the world." Wiggle Anthony Field then emceed the ceremony, which featured several other speakers, stirring musical tributes, clips from interviews and Steve's shows (including hilarious outtakes), and heartfelt videotaped testimonials by the likes of Justin Timberlake, Kelly Ripa, and Steve's mate Russell Crowe. Of those who spoke, only one got a standing ovation—and before she had even said a word. The very sight of little Bindi, walking onstage in Irwin signature khakis and piece of paper in hand, was enough to instantly bring the audience to its feet. She proceeded to deliver a speech she had written herself, in which she expressed that she didn't want "Daddy's passion to ever end" and vowed to "help wildlife just like he did." So poignant was the scene that it was voted "Television Moment of the Year" in an Australian viewers' poll.

Though Bindi was the youngest family member to speak that morning, she had not been the first. Another Irwin, one who had known Steve since his arrival on his beloved mum's birthday 44 years before, had offered brief but resounding words as well. "Please do not grieve for Steve, he's at peace now," Bob Irwin, the crocodile hunter's dad and own hero, asked of the crowd. "But I'd like you to grieve for the animals. The animals have lost the best friend they ever had, and so have I."

"Let Bindi Have the Limelight"

I do not think of myself as a celebrity, but I do think I am a teacher. It's not about 'look at me, I'm so great,' I don't think like that at all. It's about getting people to take responsibility for keeping our animals safe and protected.

—Bindi Irwin

For his family, Steve Irwin's death was more than a tragic loss. It was a massive shake-up of every aspect of their lives. At the helm of an empire, Steve had embodied the very term *wildlife conservation*. Now, his wife, daughter, and son were left to continue the mission he had always led. The public eye fell, in particular, on Bindi Irwin, who had begun to come into her own as a young conservationist. Her "incredible genes," to quote Steve, were already obvious—and now they were about to shine.

DAWNING OF A NEW G'DAY

Spring is known as a time of rebirth, and in many ways, the Australian spring of 2006 was just that—a new birth. In Australia, spring begins in September, so for the Irwins, the new season began with unspeakable sadness. As the dust settled, though, a new beginning slowly and steadily took shape. To start fresh with hearts so badly broken was incredibly difficult, but it was also necessary. Terri and the kids were determined to do it for their supporters and fans, for wildlife everywhere and, of course, for Steve.

As one important being left Bindi's life, another entered it. He certainly wasn't larger than life like her dad had been. In fact, he wasn't very large at all. That's because Candy, as eight-year-old Bindi named her newly acquired companion, was a rat. "I got him two weeks after my dad died," Bindi wrote on her personal zoo blog, *Bindi's Say.* "He helps me feel lots better!" (She went on to explain that by the time she found out Candy was a boy, he would not respond to any other name.) A sense of security is critical for any grieving child, and Bindi, naturally, had found it in an animal—one who'd sit on her shoulder as she'd rollerblade and on her lap during interviews. As she prepared to take on life without Dad, a small friend provided big comfort.

January 2007 was an important month for Bindi and her family. It marked, of course, the start of the first full year of their lives without Steve. It was also time for *G'Day USA,* the annual promotional tour that had Steve announcing plans and dreams for his family and his mission just the year before. Now, it was Terri who had been asked to be an Australian tourism ambassador. The Irwins were in high demand in the United States, where their popularity was most immense, and the time felt right. Terri and the kids headed to America.

Bindi was, by now, not only a warrior but also a budding songstress, and the Irwins' part in the tour centered around her live performances. With backup group the *Crocmen,* she performed in Los Angeles and New York, singing lively, choreographed songs about the plight of threatened wildlife. The concerts reunited Bindi

Bindi performs with The Crocmen during the G'Day USA Aussie Family Concert held at the New York City Center in January 2007.

with fellow Aussie entertainers The Wiggles, with whom she shared a headline. "It's very cool because everyone's cheering and it feels really nice to get out there and just be me and just do what I love to do, sing and dance," Bindi said on the set of ABC's *Good Morning America,* one of several stops on her talk show circuit that week. "It's really hard to explain but it's a great feeling."

Of course, the whirlwind U.S. visit wasn't all song and dance. The 10-day adventure wrapped up with the honor of a lifetime, as Bindi had been invited to speak with her mother at the Washington National Press Club luncheon in Washington, D.C. Past speakers include Winston Churchill, Indira Gandhi, and Nelson Mandela, all respected leaders with whom Bindi now had a shared experience. "They certainly are a little different," then Press Club President Jerry Zremski said of the Irwins. "We have never had an

(continues on page 80)

TO SIR WITH LOVE:
THE IRWINS HONOR A LEGEND

When asked about his greatest influences, Steve would usually start with his own mom and dad. There were others, though—legendary naturalists whom Steve had watched bring wildlife into people's homes and hearts when he was just a kid. One was, of course, Jacques Cousteau, the man who essentially defined the oceanographic documentary. Another was a man named Sir David Attenborough.

Great Britain's Attenborough, who earned the title "Sir" when he was knighted in 1985, was a pioneer in nature programming. At the start of his decades-long career with the British Broadcasting Corporation (BBC), he created *Zoo Quest,* a now-classic wildlife documentary series that ran from 1954–1964. He then spent several years on the business side of broadcast (including a stint as BBC's Director of Programmes) before deciding that inside four walls just wasn't where he belonged. He turned down a promotion to director general in favor of a return to his true passion—filming in the wild. He went on to make dozens of widely watched series and specials, including his famous 1979 series *Life on Earth,* and its sequels *The Living Planet* and the *Trials of Life.* As of 2007, he wasn't done yet. "At the moment, I'm writing about courtship in rattlesnakes, which, as you know, is very interesting," Attenborough, then 81, said in an interview for the United Kingdom's *The Observer* newspaper. "I know exactly what I want to get, what concept it's got to introduce and how it links to the next sequence."

It's no wonder Steve Irwin would count such a man among his idols. Though Attenborough is more a fascinated filmmaker than a rugged rescuer, his life's work, Steve would likely say, makes him a wildlife warrior in his own right. "He's like the voice of God," Steve said of Attenborough, known for his powerful narration, in a 2003 BBC interview.

Sir David Attenborough poses with Terri Irwin after receiving the Special Recognition Award at the United Kingdom's National Television Awards on October 31, 2010.

Terri shared her husband's admiration with Attenborough and the world when she made a surprise appearance at the British National Television Awards in 2006. She was there, on behalf of Steve, to present Attenborough with a prestigious Lifetime Achievement Award. "I promised I wasn't going to cry," she said, tearfully, in her first appearance outside of Australia since her husband's death. "But I'm especially pleased to be here, because if there's one person that directly inspired my husband it's this man." The respect, it seemed, was mutual. "He taught [people] how wonderful and exciting [the natural world] was," Sir Attenborough later said of Steve. "He was a born communicator."

(*continued from page 77*)

eight-year-old girl speak at the National Press Club, as far as I know. I can never remember anyone close to being that young. And the topic too is certainly sort of different." The Press Club focuses on issues that are of most importance to the world at any given time. That the Irwins had been chosen to speak was testament that they, including Steve, had succeeded in their goal: letting people know that wildlife conservation is as urgent an international issue as any other. In addition, the Press Club and the rest of world now knew that Bindi Irwin could deliver a great speech.

The young naturalist didn't disappoint at the January 19 conference. After Terri told attendees about the Steve she knew and loved, his dreams for wildlife protection, and the Irwin family's determination to continue his work, it was Bindi's turn to take the podium. With conviction and poise, she offered her perspective on the topic that had defined her eight years to date. "It's very sad, but in my lifetime, a lot of wildlife could disappear," she said. "We could lose tigers, gorillas, and even my favorite koalas could become extinct. We need to continue my daddy's work and make this place safer for animals."

BINDI'S JOURNEY SHARED

Steve used to say he didn't want to be a star, but rather Bindi's costar. In fact, he told his wife, he would have been all too happy to "take it easy and run the zoo, do my conservation work, and let Bindi have the limelight." Now, albeit in a way that no one would have wanted, his wish was coming true—but not without typical media scrutiny.

Some people wondered whether Bindi was reentering the spotlight too soon after her dad's death, a notion that Terri had addressed early on. "A while after Steve died I went to talk to a psychologist because the kids were handling themselves so well," Terri told *Jetstar* magazine in 2008. "I asked him if it was normal for kids to cope with grief in such a positive way and he said 'that's what we aim for.' That made me feel so proud of them." Observations of others who knew Bindi best seemed to support the professional advice. "I think she's doing great," Discovery Channel executive producer Wendy Douglas told the Australian Broadcasting Corporation in January 2007. "She's fine . . . and I really hope that people, you know, hear that when I say—and when other people who are close to her [say]—she's having the time of her life because she does want to share with people singing and dancing about animals and about respecting them . . . that's what she really, truly loves doing." As Wes Mannion, Steve's longtime best mate and director of Australia Zoo, put it: "She's a little rock."

So how did Bindi actually feel? When asked, as she often was in those first months, how she was doing, she would respond that she has "good days and bad days. Sometimes it brings back memories and it's really nice and some days I just cry straight off." As to whether she felt like touring and performing even as she mourned her dad, it indeed seemed there was nothing she felt like doing more. If anything, she indicated, thoughts of her father only drove her. "I think about him just looking at me," she said on *Good Morning America*. "Like at the dinner table and stuff, he used to say, 'Oh, Bindi, I'm so proud of you, good job, well done.' It was really nice."

Soon after the G'Day trip, *Ocean's Deadliest* aired on the Discovery Channel as planned. It featured Steve, but it didn't star him—a precursor to an upcoming wildlife program that would do the same: his daughter's show. *Bindi the Jungle Girl,* on hold since Steve died, had resumed production and premiered on Discovery Kids on June 9, 2007. (The evening before, the network aired an hour-long program hosted by Bindi called *My Daddy the Crocodile Hunter,* where viewers saw Steve impart to his daughter his love for wildlife through specially selected footage.) The format of *Bindi the Jungle Girl* did more to fulfill Steve's dream to being Bindi's sidekick. Though it would be the younger Irwin's show, original plans for Steve to be a major part of it stayed intact. "We'll never refer to the fact that Steve's no longer with us," producer Stainton told *People* magazine. "The way that it works is that Steve plays costar to Bindi." The crew had shot 7 of the ultimate 26 episodes before Steve's death.

The premise of the show, which still airs on the network, has Bindi living up in a tree house in the middle of the jungle with more than half a dozen of her favorite creatures. Among them are an iguana, a cockatoo, a koala, a snake—and a toddler. "Over there is where my brother lives," Bindi says during her animal introductions on the premiere, and the camera cuts to a giggling three-year-old Robert. Candy is a part-time resident, and other animals, she explains, "come and go." From the tree house, Bindi shows viewers these various visitors from the wild, offers up interesting facts, and introduces the videotaped segments. These, including one called "Croc Hunter Unplugged," generally feature Steve, Wes, the zoo staff, and often Bindi as they encounter all walks of wildlife from around "Bindi's Globe." Music videos in which the Crocmen and/or Bindi perform are another regular part of the show, and splashy, animated graphics and sound effects add to the overall appeal of each episode.

Although song, dance, animals, and a pint-sized host alone are an easy recipe for children's approval, parents and critics can be tougher sells. They look for valuable messages packaged inside original, creative fun—and find it in *Bindi the Jungle Girl*. One mom who is also a reviewer for Common Sense Media, a nonprofit organization dedicated to helping families choose media wisely, had this to say:

> Parents need to know that this educational series—which focuses on Crocodile Hunter Steve Irwin's daughter Bindi—is a great choice for the whole family. The spunky young hostess is just as passionate about wildlife as her famous dad, and catchy song-and-dance numbers add to the learning in a fun, kid-friendly way. Viewers of all ages will come away with a new appreciation for nature's diversity and be reminded of the importance of preserving animals' natural habitats.

Bindi had arrived. Between animals and the camera, it seemed a tossup as to which loved her more. Now it was clear to the world what her friends and family had known for a long time: She was undoubtedly, as *People* had stated, "a chip off the old croc."

THE BUSINESS OF BINDI

Bindi's most natural mode of conservation promotion seemed to be TV, just as her dad's had been. Home video worked well, too, as demonstrated through her debut on *Wiggly Safari* and, in 2006, on an animal-themed workout DVD called *Bindi KidFitness*. On the best-selling DVD, Bindi and the Crocmen taught young viewers about exercise and nutrition to the tune of their own fun songs while Steve cooked up some healthy snacks. After the splash they made with *Jungle Girl,* Bindi and her backup boys even tried their hand at hip-hop when they released the single "Trouble in the Jungle" on November 15, 2007 (the second annual Steve Irwin Day). They were invited to perform the tune live on the *Today* show that month. Bindi's ongoing success in the media made sense. "As soon as I was born I was in front of the camera," she told *TV Guide.* "I feel like I've got a place there." Despite that comfort zone, Bindi was ready and excited to do more. She was thrilled with her next project, one in which she'd get to wear her heart—or at least her conservation message—on her sleeve.

Everyone knows the Irwins have a way with wildlife, but few might realize that the family also boasts a member with a flair for fashion. In 2000, Bindi's aunt Joy Muscillo (Steve's sister), with Queensland designers Palmina Distasi and Melanie Berry, started Bindi Wear, a range of kids' clothing inspired by wildlife. Though available exclusively through Australia Zoo (even today), this original line became the seed for something bigger. In August 2007, soon after *Bindi the Jungle Girl* took off, Bindi entered a different kind of wild world: the fashion industry. Bindi Wear International, an expanded line under the management of 3 Monsters, LLC, made its catwalk debut at Magic, a major Las Vegas trade show that regularly hosts brands such as Nike, Calvin Klein, Baby Phat, and Sean John.

They shared an impressive venue, but a lot sets Bindi Wear International apart from those big names. Dubbed as "clothes with a conscience," Bindi's line, which includes shirts, shorts, skirts, swimwear, and accessories, has tags made of recycled cardboard, and the shoes also have soles made with recycled rubber. Although the use of eco-friendly materials does send a message, one is also printed on each clothing item itself. "It's been so much fun being able to create these gorgeous clothes that have a great conservation message," Bindi told *JetStar* magazine in 2008. "Some of the sayings on the clothes are 'Save It' and 'Tigers should be loved, not rugs.' I was involved in the designing and I also wrote the messages by hand." Also unlike a typical fashion line, Bindi Wear International could be called one big fashion-forward fundraiser. "Every dollar goes back into conservation," Terri states in a promotional video on the label's Web site. "It's not a percentage—all of it." Bindi Wear International was made available at select stores in Australia in March of the following year and in the United States soon after.

At age nine, Bindi had certainly reached, if not surpassed, the point at which kids start to care about what they wear. Girls, in particular, might even welcome clothes as gifts, so long as they're from a "tween-savvy" shopper. Many of Bindi's fans, though, weren't there yet. They were still at an age where toys rule—and Bindi had something in store for them, too. In June 2008, the latest Bindi-inspired merchandise was introduced at the New York Toy Fair, the equivalent to Vegas's Magic for the world of fun and games. It was *Wild Republic's* Bindi doll, a 10-inch-tall (25.4-cm-tall) likeness of Bindi sporting khakis and fluffy pigtails like hers. The standard mini-Bindi also comes with a few friends, including a wombat, a python, and a cockatoo. Various versions of the doll, including Rainforest Rescue, Rainforest Adventure, and Ocean and Surf, are available, but the coolest part for many young Bindi fans is likely that some dolls actually talk. (Messages include "Crikey! Let's go help wildlife" and "You can make the world a better place," among others.) A portion of the proceeds from the Bindi doll goes to conservation projects.

Stage, screen, fashion, or toys, the business of Bindi, she and her family maintained, always came down to one thing only: "It's got to be about wildlife conservation and it's got to be benefiting conservation," Terri told Australian talk show host Andrew Denton in October 2007. If her daughter wasn't doing more, it certainly wasn't for a

Bindi and Robert present the New Wild Republic, Bindi's toy line, at FAO Schwarz in New York City on February 18, 2008.

A FOUNDING FATHER'S FAREWELL

There was a time when a family of four could drop $1.30 and spend an afternoon observing Australia's small reptiles in a safe and natural habitat. Since then, Bob Irwin had seen his humble Beerwah Reptile Park grow from a very local attraction to the most popular tourist destination in the country. In March 2008, nearly four decades after starting it all, he was ready to hang up his hat.

As his granddaughter happily sustained the family's television empire, Australia Zoo's cofounder (with his wife, Lyn, in 1970) made a highly publicized decision to leave the family business. Though his reasons weren't perfectly clear to the public, Irwin said on the biographical program *Australian Story* that he "just felt that it was better for everybody concerned." Yet the resignation happened soon after claims of possible trouble within the extended Irwin family. The general theme was Bob's alleged feeling that Terri was commercializing the zoo. A specific disagreement, unnamed sources told the magazine *New Idea,* related to the future of a koala project at Iron Bark Station, the zoo's rehabilitation facility, where Bob lived. Both sides denied any family rift, although a 300-word statement that Bob gave the media raised eyebrows. In it, he thanked zoo staff, animal hospital workers, Wildlife Warriors, and "all Steve's friends out there," notably leaving out Terri and her contributions. His plan

lack of interested parties who saw her as highly marketable. "Bindi is lucky in that opportunities come in thick and fast—and they are turned down thick and fast," Terri said in an interview with the U.K.'s *TimesOnline* that same month. "You don't see Bindi endorsing some fast-food restaurant or a new trendy anything, because she's a kid . . . we're Wildlife Warriors."

was to move to a smaller property and carry out conservation projects there. "You may rest assured that Judy [his partner] and I will continue Steve's dream, with the passion and commitment he would expect," he stated. "Steve's ultimate passion, even from a young boy, was always for the conservation of Australian wildlife and its habitat."

Wes Mannion told the media that Bob had not been involved in the zoo's general management for years. He had left its board in 2003 and was primarily managing Iron Bark Station. If her father-in-law's departure and the talk that surrounded it had caused any hard feelings, Terri never let on. "There's no rift and I love Bob," she said on the Australian current-affairs show *Today Tonight.* "He's done a wonderful job of managing one of our conservation properties. After everything he's suffered, I think a gentleman of retirement age deserves some privacy and to be able to live his life how he sees fit." Incidentally, he would later experience a different kind of suffering: Bob had a major heart attack in April 2010. Recovering at home on his conservation property with Judy (now his wife), he told *The Courier-Mail* he'd received an outpouring of support, much of it from strangers. Although he'd need to take it a bit easier, Bob indicated, he planned to keep up his lifelong crusade. "I've been very, very fortunate," he said. "It was a real wake-up call."

"AND THE WINNER IS . . ."

In true Irwin tradition, Bindi had won countless fans by simply doing what she loved: spreading the conservation message in ways that would reach people best. Every celebrity knows that with popularity comes the awards circuit, and on two continents, Bindi was no exception.

It had begun in the United States where Bindi was invited to take part in the Nickelodeon Kids' Choice Awards in April 2007. She had the honor of helping present the award for Favorite Male Singer to Justin Timberlake. A month later, Bindi had the role of presenter again, this time back in her homeland at the annual TV Week Logie Awards. There, Bindi presented the award for Most Outstanding Children's series, which went to *The Upside Down*

Terri and Bindi Irwin pose with Bindi's two awards at the Nickelodeon Australian Kids' Choice Awards on October 11, 2007.

Show. All of this, of course, was before the premiere of *Bindi the Jungle Girl,* so the world mainly knew Bindi as Steve Irwin's courageous and conservation-conscious little girl. Those who had seen *KidFitness* or any of her tour were also aware that she could sing and dance. After the American summer of 2007, though, she'd find herself on the other side of award presentations. In October, it was time for the Nickelodeon Australian Kids' Choice Awards. Whether her breakout TV show was responsible or not, one thing was made clear that night: Aussie kids love Bindi. She won Biggest Greenie and the ultimate honor—Fave Aussie. Others who took signature orange blimps that evening included Zac Efron, Pink, The Veronicas, and *Australian Idol.*

May 2008 brought the fiftieth annual Logie Awards in Melbourne, and the Irwin camp was in attendance once again—this time, a contender among them. Bindi was up for Most Popular New Talent—Female, and her Australia Zoo family could not have been prouder. "What a huge achievement for our nine-year-old Wildlife Warrior!" reads an archived message, referring to the nomination alone, on the zoo's Web site from that March. On her zoo blog, Bindi describes the experience of walking the red carpet with her mum that evening, and the unmatched joy of what happened soon after. "All the categories came up, but then mine did! They said all these top actresses' names then my name! The guy said 'And the winner is . . .' . . . My heart stopped . . . 'Bindi Irwin!' I could not believe it, I WON! I was amazed, in tears, I could hardly talk! I'll never forget that great trip!"

Another unforgettable trip was just around the corner. The following month, it was back to the United States, by now Bindi's home away from home. What made this jaunt to Los Angeles unlike any other, however, was the reason for it: Bindi had been nominated for not one, but several, Daytime Emmy Awards. More than that, she stood to make television history, as she'd be the youngest Daytime Emmy Award winner ever if she scored an award. On June 20, 2008, at the famed Kodak Theatre (home of *American Idol,* among other events) in Los Angeles, history happened. Weeks shy of ten, Bindi Irwin was presented with the coveted golden statue for Outstanding Performer in a Children's Series. She expressed amazement at having won out over her experienced competitors and gratitude for *Bindi the Jungle Girl*'s staggering U.S. success over such a short time period. What she was most grateful for, though, was the life she got to live every day. "I am the luckiest kid in the world!" she told the media. "I live in a zoo and I get to teach other kids about animals in a fun way—what more could you want?"

Land and Sea

I always thought being Steve's right-hand woman was my des-
tiny. That everything I'd been groomed for in my life had led to
this point. And then I realized it wasn't. I'd been groomed for
after Steve was gone.

—Terri Irwin

After Steve's death, Terri's main focus was twofold. Naturally, she wanted to ensure the happiness and well-being of their children. She also wanted, as a family, to continue her husband's mission the best they could. Certainly Steve would want to keep showing the world how exciting and important its creatures are, and on that front, Bindi had quickly and successfully stepped in. Still, the family knew that there was much more to wildlife conservation than what a person could catch on TV—and it wasn't always easy.

HUNTED

The animals closest to Steve's heart were clearly the ones that ruled the Outback's rivers and swamps. In his later years, however, the crocodile hunter had gained increased interest in wildlife that inhabited the world's larger bodies of water: its oceans. His 2004 Antarctica trip had given him a new appreciation for sea creatures and intensified his drive to do more for them. He was particularly concerned about humpback whales, an endangered species that was being slowly destroyed in the name of "research." Japanese fleets regularly kill these gentle giants of the sea in order, they claim, to study them, a practice still technically legal due to a loophole in current laws. "They run them down with their ships, with a gunner up the front," Steve answered when interviewer Larry King asked him in 2004 how the whales are killed. "And believe me, when you're being hunted . . . the fear that you feel, like I got goose bumps, mate, because it just drives me nuts. The fear of being hunted is a fear that I hope most people never ever face." According to antiwhaling activists, not only is killing unnecessary for whale research, but the main purpose of these fleets is to support the whale-meat trade.

Steve had been seriously considering joining forces with Sea Shepherd Conservation Society (SSCS), whose primary mission is to defend the lives of whales and other marine animals. The organization got its start in Terri's home state of Oregon in 1981, and now has 10 offices worldwide in addition to its Washington State headquarters. A year after Steve's death, SSCS sought Terri's blessing to give her husband the highest honor by renaming one of its two flagships for him. Terri readily gave her support, and on December 5, 2007, the former *Robert Hunter* officially became the *Steve Irwin*. "Steve Irwin's life demonstrated how one person can make a significant difference in the world," Captain Paul Watson, the group's founder and president, said at a press conference to announce the renaming. "Steve wanted to come to Antarctica with us to defend the whales and now he is able to join us in spirit with his name emblazoned on the fastest and most powerful whale protection ship

A WORTHY NAMESAKE

Though Steve Irwin is gone from our world, his name lives on through the many things—living and nonliving—that bear his name. The first was introduced back in 1997, when Steve and his dad discovered a new species of snapping turtle during a fishing trip. Given the honor of choosing a name for the species, Steve called it *Elseya irwini* (Irwin's turtle). Since Steve's death, several organizations in addition to SSCS have honored Steve by naming something precious after him. The following are Irwin-inspired creatures, places, and things that exist today:

- In June 2007, the Rwandan government named a baby gorilla after Steve in its third annual gorilla-naming ceremony. The young primate's name is Ingufu Steve Irwin, which means "strength and energy of Steve Irwin."
- Animal Planet renamed the garden in front of the Discovery Channel's Maryland headquarters the Steve Irwin Memorial Sensory Garden soon after Steve's death.
- On January 1, 2007, Glasshouse Mountains Road, which runs past Australia Zoo, was officially renamed Steve Irwin Way.
- The Queensland Museum named a rare snail species discovered in the state's mountainous regions *Crikey steveirwini* in November 2009. Said museum scientist Dr. John Stanisic of his decision to honor Steve: "It was the [snail's] khaki colour that immediately drew the connection to the late Crocodile Hunter."
- In 2009, Australia's Perth Mint unveiled a one-dollar Steve Irwin coin as part of its Inspirational Australians series. The tender bears the conservationist's name, the years of his birth and death, and his likeness, surrounded by several animals. On the front of the coin, naturally, is the crocodile.

in the world." In its first official voyage as an honorary Irwin, the ship soon set off for Operation Migaloo, an antiwhaling effort in the Southern Oceans (a recently named area where the Pacific, Indian, and Atlantic Oceans meet).

SSCS, whose logo is an angry-looking skull perched above a shepherd's staff crossed over a pitchfork, has not been without controversy in its three decades of existence. This is because its main conservation method is to directly intervene with Japanese whaling operations on the high seas. This intervention often involves physical collisions between SSCS's boats and the whalers' boats, and authorities have entered the picture on numerous occasions. (In one case, a crew for a new Animal Planet show called *Whale Wars* was there when Australian police officers boarded an SSCS vessel and seized several items, including videotapes.) Captain Watson himself has long been at odds with Greenpeace, the legendary environmentalist group which, ironically, he helped create in 1972. They once called him an "ecoterrorist," though Watson maintains that the watery confrontations of the SSCS do not cause injury. Watson's organization has also gained official support from a slew of celebrities, including Mick Jagger, Uma Thurman, the Dalai Lama, Martin Sheen, and Pierce Brosnan, to name a small sampling. Then there are Terri, Bindi, and Robert Irwin, who made a surprise bon-voyage visit before the SSCS crew disembarked for Operation Waltzing Matilda in December 2009. The ship heading out that day was, of course, the *Steve Irwin*.

WHALE OF A TALE

The formal bond with the SSCS was only one of the Irwins' many whale-focused adventures during that early difficult time. In fact, one of the first things that Terri, Bindi, Robert, and the Australia Zoo management had decided to do after Steve's death was introduce a whale-watching program at the zoo. They acquired a new boat that they named *Steve's Whale One,* on which zoo visitors could see, appreciate, and hopefully learn to love the serene and friendly humpbacks that inhabit Australia's coastal waters. As Steve had always taught, conservation begins in the hearts of people.

Bindi the Jungle Girl viewers got to see, through a videotaped segment, the family's official launch of the new boat on an episode called "Saving the Whales." As its title implies, the episode was dedicated to the plight of these animals, and it was a perfect venue for Bindi to give the world an exclusive preview of her latest project. She had recorded a song called "Save Me," an emotional plea for help in the "voice" of the whales themselves. Musical interludes feature humpback whales' own actual songs, the melancholy moaning and howling sounds that the species is known to make. The music video shows actual footage of whale attacks playing behind Bindi as she sings. Bindi's primary purpose was to show people in Asia, where she planned to release the song and video, what is happening with hopes of inspiring citizens to push for change. Whether or not she made an impact in the Far East, she had clearly made one in the United States. One of her 2008 Daytime Emmy Award nominations was in the category of Outstanding Original Song. "I really love whales and we should do our best to protect them," Bindi said, as reported by the *Herald Sun* in June 2008. "'Save Me' is all about how precious these beautiful animals are."

Incidentally, Bindi's musical endeavor served as a fitting soundtrack for an exciting project that her mom was starting at around the same time. In January 2008, Terri and the Marine Mammal Institute at Oregon State University announced that they would launch a year-plus study of several whale species throughout the world's oceans. Made possible through grants from Terri, the high-tech project would show that researchers can gather key information on the animals' populations, habitats, and behaviors in humane ways. "We can actually learn everything the Japanese are learning with lethal research by using nonlethal research," Terri told Australia's Channel 9 (as reported by *The Courier-Mail*), speaking of a method that uses satellite-monitored radio tagging to track the whales. Bindi accompanied her mother and Marine Mammal Institute director Bruce Mate, who pioneered the tagging technique, on a research

Bindi promoted her movie *Free Willy: Escape from Pirate's Cove* around the world. Here, she and her mother pose during a press event at the Toronto Zoo in Canada in March 2010.

trip that September. "The device we used to tag them sort of looked like a gun, but don't worry, it wasn't," she wrote in *Bindi's Say*. "With pressure of air it punched the tag into the whale so that only the antenna stuck up. The antenna had to stick up so that we could get the information back. We get information every time the whale takes a breath."

Armed with that hard-to-find combination of star quality and marine-mammal savvy, Bindi seemed perfect for what would be her next project. Hollywood filmmakers had once knocked on the crocodile hunter's door; now they had an offer for his daughter. In 2008, Bindi accepted the starring role in *Free Willy: Escape from Pirate's Cove*, the fourth installment in the film series that began with the 1993 now-classic film *Free Willy*. In the straight-to-DVD film, Bindi would play Kirra Cooper, a young animal lover who goes to live with her estranged grandfather, Gus (played by veteran actor Beau Bridges). When Gus decides to keep a trapped baby orca as an attraction for his seaside amusement park, Kirra knows she must take action. Bindi was off to South Africa to start filming in February 2009, and the film was released in March 2010. "You know, I watched my dad's movie so many times, *Crocodile Hunter: Collision Course*, I actually said to my mom that one day I'd love to do a movie," Bindi said in an interview with online teen magazine *J-14*. "When *Free Willy* came along and they asked if I wanted to do this movie of course we said yes because it's not just a fun, action-packed family movie but you'll also accidentally learn something while you're watching it."

TROUBLE IN THE WETLANDS

Being world-renowned conservationists requires covering a lot of ground—often acres on acres of the swampy variety. As whale wars waged off the coasts of Antarctica and Australia, the Irwins had other problems to confront back in the Outback. The trouble was with the Steve Irwin Wildlife Reserve, a section of 333,592 acres (135,000 hectares) of land on the Cape York Peninsula. In 2007, the Australian government had given the Irwins funds to buy the property to be designated as "a permanent memorial managed by the Irwin family trust for environmental purposes to fulfill Steve's vision that we can conserve and protect Australia's special environments by acquiring it and preserving it forever," Environment Minister Malcolm Turnbull had explained on announcing plans for the purchase.

Months later, conflict arose when the family learned that mining company Cape Alumina had applied to mine bauxite (a type of sedimentary rock that yields aluminum oxide used to make a variety of products) on a small part of the land. Terri and Bindi

WORLDWIDE CLASSROOM

Some people might think that days filled with filmmaking, whale tagging, and jungle tree-house living equal a free pass out of studying. To those people, Bindi would say, "Think again!" Schooling has been a major, steady part of Bindi's life and career since she was old enough to start it. Homeschooled after a year of formal preschool ("she cried every day, so we stole the teacher," Terri quipped to Larry King in 2007), Bindi studies at home and anywhere else she happens to be. Her "stolen" teacher, Emma, regularly travels with the family, and the two are "really good friends," Bindi told Larry King. She also said her favorite subject was creative writing, and her least favorite, as King had guessed, was math.

Not only is schoolwork part of Bindi's (and now Bob's) life, but as with any other kid, it comes first. "While [the kids] are filming, they have a teacher that runs around after them with flashcards," Terri told Australian talk show host Andrew Denton in 2007. "Bindi has a solid three hours of home school before doing anything."

promptly launched a campaign they called "Save Steve's Place," which involved legal action and two online petitions to fight the company's plans. "I am not a woman who is against mining or against compromise but in this particular area it is impossible to compromise," Terri announced. "The removal of the bauxite would destroy all of the plant species growing on it. It would be irreparable so there could be no compromise with this particular area." Cape Alumina chief executive Paul Messenger indicated there would be no problem because the company had "no plans to mine any wetlands, springs or rivers or any other areas with high conservation values." He also maintained (and news sources reported) that Cape

Bindi's adventurous schedule doesn't preclude run-of-the-mill activities, either. Added Terri: "Her school day always includes extra-curricular things like swimming, mixed martial arts, cooking lessons, piano lessons, surfing, horseback riding." People who question or criticize the practice of home schooling often focus on the social aspect, as many homeschooled kids don't have the regular exposure to peers that other kids do. It's an issue that both Bindi and Terri consider, well, a nonissue. Bindi and her friend Rosie, whom she met in preschool, still hang out whenever they can. "We would stick up for each other and we got on really well," Bindi told *Jetstar* magazine in 2008. "When I decided to do home schooling, we still remained really good friends. She's great—we do stuff together . . . horse riding, paint our nails, do our hair."

On top of all the standard things, Bindi gets the benefit of something few other kids do: the coolest natural science class anyone could imagine. She lives it every day—and she wouldn't change a thing. As she told *Jetstar,* "I am living my dream and doing what I love."

Alumina held exploration permits on the land before the Irwins bought it, but the Irwins insisted the statement was flat-out false. As with most legal battles, the two sides' take on the issue seemed to completely contradict one another, and each held on firmly to its own opinion.

"WE CAN'T DO NOTHING"

If it's important to Bindi, it has an entry in *Bindi's Say,* and the campaign to save her dad's land was no exception. In August 2008, she described a crocodile-catching trip to the disputed area, which was also her very first visit there. "It was like walking into a fairy-land," she wrote. "But instead of fairies there were butterflies and dragonflies and birds!" She went on to describe how bauxite mining destroys habitats ("the springs are made up of bauxite and if you take it out there will be no water left") and asked readers to sign the petition on the zoo's Web site. The following April, the family's plight gained major exposure when actor Russell Crowe publicly declared his support. "[Irwin is] not here to stand up for himself and I just feel, as his friend, that we can't do [nothing]," Crowe said on the *Late Show with David Letterman.* "It is a global irresponsibility to do that." Though Crowe's appearance resulted in an instant boost for the petition—more than 13,000 people immediately added signatures—Cape Alumina seemed unrattled. "I think Steve Irwin had many friends and some of them are high-profile people who are entitled to their opinion," Messenger said, adding a reminder that the company had no plans to disrupt rivers or wetland areas.

In August 2009, another high-profile supporter, one known as an environmental crusader, joined the Irwins' campaign. Erin Brockovich was a legal clerk in the mid-1990s when she uncovered wrong-doings by a major California utilities company, leading to a hugely successful lawsuit. Brockovich rose to international fame when actress Julia Roberts starred in a 2000 movie based on her fascinating story. A sought-after environmental legal consultant since her landmark case, Brockovich specifically named the younger Irwin when she announced her support. "I'm helping Bindi with her plight in what's going on out there," she said.

In December 2009, the campaign experienced a setback when Queensland Minister for Mines and Energy Stephen Robertson denied the Irwins' petition. He wrote that he would follow the usual environmental impact statement in assessing Cape Alumina's applications to mine the land. It would take more than denial of a petition, however, to stop the Irwins and their hundreds of thousands of supporters. As of April 2010, the Wilderness Society of Australia had officially joined the campaign and had spearheaded a new focus. Terri, Bindi, and the group were urging the Queensland government to accept a proposed declaration that would protect a major river basin on the reserve, in turn, severely limiting any legal mining there. Though Cape Alumina called the new attention to the campaign "the latest political stunt," the Irwins seem highly unlikely to be deterred. "This area is vital in maintaining water flow and habitat to significant flora and fauna," Terri said in a statement when the first petition was denied. "There is no argument. We need to stand as a nation, a state, a community to protect wildlife and wild places for our children." Somewhere, the original wildlife warrior surely seconded that.

Everything
Steve Believed In

I watched this very, very old movie and it had a line in it that went, "Children should be seen and not heard." . . . Back then kids didn't get to have an opinion. They didn't get to speak for themselves. I think it's so important because we are that next generation taking care of our planet.

—Bindi Irwin

Nearly half a decade later, those who knew and loved Steve Irwin may still shake their heads in mournful disbelief. Tune in to the Discovery Kids TV channel or watch an online clip and the crocodile hunter seems, in all his animal-loving vibrancy, to live again. While gone from our midst, he carries on in a way that gives new meaning to the term *legacy*. Every hero leaves one but rarely in the form of a fiercely driven family whose spirit, ideals, and goals exactly match his own. As an eight-year-old Bindi told talk show host Ellen DeGeneres in early 2007, "My dad really brought out 'me.' He's the one that *made* me." The best way to secure your legacy, Steve might advise, is to nurture, teach, and cherish it before you go.

AUSSIE FOREVER

When Terri Irwin moved halfway around the world to start a life with her new husband, she intended to stay. The tragic loss of her soul mate 14 years later did nothing to change that intention; in fact, she resolved to solidify it. As Steve's wife and the surviving parent of their children, she'd need to take every measure to help reinforce the Irwin family's sense of place and purpose. One such measure, simple yet profound, was to formally declare her own.

After Steve was gone, some naturally wondered about the future of Australia Zoo and Terri's plans in general. Speculation hit a particular high around the time that the elder Bob Irwin left the zoo in light of unconfirmed reports that he felt the family's conservation empire was becoming too commercial. There were rumors that Terri might return to the United States mixed with other rumors that she planned to turn the zoo into a theme park—ideas that Terri consistently tried to put to rest. "I'll never leave," she told *Today Tonight* in 2008. "I love Australia and I'm doing my best to be a fair dinkum Aussie sheila and honor all of Steve's work, [so] I'll be here the rest of my life." She also assured the public that the zoo would most definitely expand, but it would remain an educational zoological facility at its core. "There will sure be a lot more animals, more mega fun and more hands-on experiences," she said on the show.

Still, although Australia's Sunshine Coast had been Terri's home for more than one-third of her life and she ran its biggest attraction, there was a missing piece: She wasn't an Australian in the official sense. On November 15, 2009, to the delighted surprise of a crowd of 5,000, Terri changed that. It was the third annual Steve Irwin Day, and the Crocoseum was filled with the crocodile hunter's family, friends, and fans for the usual festivities. Little did they know that they would serve as honored witnesses to one of the Irwin family's most prized moments. With Bindi and Robert at her side, Terri

Each November, Australia Zoo celebrates Steve Irwin Day. Surrounded by staffers, Steve's father Bob, Steve's friend Wes Mannion, Bindi, Robert, and Terri celebrate Steve's favorite themes—fun, family, and wildlife—in November 2007.

took an oath to become an Australian citizen in a ceremony led by Queensland Senator Mark Furner. The three Irwins then led the crowd in a rendition of "Advance Australia Fair," the land's national anthem. Although Terri Irwin was already "a true-blue Aussie," Wes Mannion had told visitors in his introduction to the ceremony, she now joined her family in their official status. In *Steve & Me,* Terri had called Bindi's demonstrated desire to continue her dad's work "a testament to everything Steve believed in." This moment, those who watched it would likely agree, was another.

YOUNG ROOS SPREAD THE NEWS

Bindi could not believe her ears when she heard someone, even a character in an old film, say that children were meant to be "seen and not heard." As she pointed out, it's "that next generation" on whom the world will depend to protect its environment. So, whose ideas, enthusiasm, and activism could be more important than those of kids? Australia Zoo Wildlife Warriors know the answer just might be no one.

In 2009, the conservation organization, founded by Steve and sponsored by Australia Zoo, established the Joey Ambassadors Program, an innovative way to let the world's youngest conservationists do the talking. Each year Wildlife Warriors will choose 12 lucky kids from around the world to actively promote wildlife conservation. The Joeys are given specific "challenges" in early October with the objective of raising a certain amount of money, along with lots of awareness, by Steve Irwin Day (November 15). The tasks, which each Joey must do individually, have ranged from placing donation boxes outside of area businesses to organizing a "Khaki Day" at one local and one international school. "Our Joey Ambassadors come from Australia, New Zealand, the United States, and Hong Kong, and are a very special group of hand-picked young people who have shown a real commitment to the cause," Wildlife Warriors Appeals Manager Murray Munro said, speaking of the program's first group, in a 2009 press release. "They epitomise [sic] the things that Steve Irwin was famous for and are the next generation to take us forward in conservation."

How did they show the type of commitment that earned them their prestigious appointment? The ways were limited only by each Joey Ambassador's imagination, knowledge, and drive. Siblings Ben and Renee Haywood (mascots: emu and red-bellied black snake) of New Zealand wowed the 2009 panel with their successful idea for the previous year's Steve Irwin Day, the country's *North Shore Times* reported. Ben told the paper they drew 130 people and raised $800 with a campout at their own home. Jacob Danko (mascot: platypus) of Pennsylvania was named a Joey Ambassador both for his long-time fundraising efforts for Wildlife Warriors and his dedication to animals in need. When he found a badly injured turtle in a local park, he gingerly brought it home, where he and his parents (based on a wildlife expert's advice) rehabilitated the animal. "When I see

CONSERVATION BY THE BOOK

Just when you think all of Bindi's talents have been tapped, she draws new inspiration from a rather unlikely source: her pet rat, Candy. Not long ago she decided to write a story about the furry sidekick that she acquired shortly after her dad's death. As it turned out, that little "rat tale" was only the beginning.

In June 2010, Bindi and Random House Australia released *Bindi Wildlife Adventures,* a book series for young readers that draws on the heroine's exciting real-life experiences. The pilot book, *Trouble at the Zoo,* has Bindi celebrating her birthday in the usual all-out style at Australia Zoo when a 10-year-old visitor plots to steal a water dragon. What happens next? As they say, you'll have to read the book. "I love to read," the budding author told *Sunshine Coast Daily,* "so I thought that these books might be another way to share with kids my love for wildlife."

To date, seven more books have followed, their plots ranging from controversy at a South African antelope sanctuary to a daring bushfire rescue in Bindi's own outback. In every case, Bindi, along with a friend or her familiar family members, seek to save animals from various threats. Whether it's an entire population or a single frightened creature on the line, the characters stop at nothing to provide help. "From the moment our . . . team first met Bindi we were struck by her genuine passion for and deep understanding of animals and the environment and her strong desire to spread the mantra of kid empowerment around the world," Linsay Knight of Random House Australia said for the *Sunshine Coast* article. That, as always, is the singular goal. As Bindi stated, "Every kid can make a difference, and I hope these books get all kids excited about changing our world."

an animal in trouble, I have to help it," Jacob told a reporter for Philadelphia-area Web news site *PhillyBurbs.com*. "Isn't that what we're supposed to do?"

Once armed with the title, Joey Ambassadors stepped up their game even more in anticipation of the upcoming November 15 celebrations. In a Steve Irwin Day site blog, Suzie Magann (mascot: kangaroo) of Hoppers Crossing, Victoria, announced her participation in Australia Zoo's "Answer the Call" campaign. She put out a request for used cell phones, which she was collecting in order to help protect gorillas in Africa. Cell phones contain coltan, she explained, which is a rare mineral that otherwise must be mined from some of the animals' last remaining natural habitats. She also reminded readers that conservation is about much more than fundraising and protecting habitat. "It is also about teaching people that we CAN live along side our wildlife . . . and we do not need to [be] fearful of them," she wrote. Although there is no one best way to help protect wildlife, Joey Ambassadors seem to agree that the worst thing a person can do is nothing. As Ben Haywood stated, "You have to be active to be a Wildlife Warrior so you have to be 'out there,' which is what we are doing."

NO PLACE LIKE HOME

While there's indeed much to be done "out there," the Irwins know there's also plenty going on at their own "right here." In 2010, Australia Zoo, both the start and the heart of the family's conservation empire, celebrated its fortieth birthday with a year of special events. Since 1970, the grounds have expanded from 4 acres (1.6 hectares) to 70 acres (28 hectares), and more than 1,000 creatures currently call the zoo home. Visitors can check out how hands-on the zoo experience has become in recent years, with opportunities to hand-feed elephants, hold koalas, and more. During school breaks, Bindi fans can take in her live

(*continues on page 110*)

WHAT ABOUT BOB?

We know Bindi. Not only was her very birth big news, but her way with both wildlife and audiences was evident early in her life. That earned the crocodile hunter's firstborn a name as a little conservationist before she could even say the word. The world knows less about her brother, the third in a line of crocodile-catching Irwin men. So just what is Robert "Baby Bob" Irwin, now seven, up to these days? As his family and kids throughout Australia would attest, he's just as wild a warrior as any.

Whether through music, film, or eco-friendly clothing tags, Bindi is clearly about getting the word out there, particularly to the population to whom she can best relate. It's a mission that Terri, in a 2010 interview with *The Courier-Mail,* called "kid empowerment— that change-your-world feeling." Meanwhile, Robert seems to have inherited the other side of his dad—that part that was far more at home in a swamp than at a black-tie gala. "Robert decided he wanted to be all about discovery," Terri told the paper. "He wants to get out there and do it and wrangle it and experience it and climb it. That's his passion. He's very (like) Steve." Given his interests, it's no wonder the younger Irwin child has his own channel on Australia Zoo TV, the zoo's Web-based network. When viewers tune in to the site (http://australiazoo.tv/) and choose "Robert's Real Life Adventures," they can see the junior activist serve alternately as star, host, commentator, and even camera man on his own wildlife "Webisodes." From New Zealand to the United States to all corners of his native Australia, Robert takes his family and, virtually, his fans on countless global adventures. He gets to see both new and favorite creatures, although never the one type he'd probably like to meet most. "I wonder if there are any dinosaurs out here," he says hopefully in one episode, shot from Tasmania's West Coast Wilderness Railway.

With guidance from his parents, Bob has always felt comfortable holding wildlife. Here, Bob and his dad Steve pose with a creature at Australia Zoo on August 2, 2006.

A month before he turned six, Robert joined Bindi at the 2009 Australian Kids' Choice Awards, where both were up for Biggest Greenie—and jointly won. Through their votes, the children of Australia had spoken, saying that no one does more to protect the

(continues)

(continued)

natural world than the crocodile hunter's two living legacies. Bindi could not have had more pride in little Robert after the win. "He's the best brother in the whole world," she wrote in a *Bindi's Say* entry. For Robert's part, this "show-biz" stuff may take some getting used to. "It's a bit loud," he told reporter Katherine Field when she asked what he thought of the hordes of fans who lined the signature orange carpet. As Steve might have said, the roar of the crowd can't hold a candle to the roar of the wild.

(continued from page 107)

performances featuring—move over, Crocmen—her new backup group, the Jungle Girls.

While there's never a dull day at Beerwah's wildlife wonderland, two in particular stand out as the least dull of all. Every year the public is invited to celebrate Bindi's and Robert's birthdays—July 24 and December 1, respectively—with awesome activities throughout the day. When Bindi turned 12, the release of her first movie inspired the party theme: star-studded, red-carpet fun. Kids got in free (a usual celebration perk) and were encouraged to "dress to impress." The Irwins and zoo staff of course went glam themselves, with Terri, Bindi, and Wes Mannion conducting croc shows in their finest attire. "We had a fantastic day," Bindi said, as reported on the zoo's Web site. "I mean, it's not every day you get to dress up in dresses at the zoo! We're usually in khakis, so we're having a fantastic time." The biggest highlight was perhaps the Crocoseum's transformation into the coolest outdoor movie theater ever for a screening of *Free Willy: Escape from Pirate's Cove,* the film at the center of it all.

As the Irwins know better than anyone, though, conservation work isn't always a party. The zoo, in cooperation with Wildlife

Warriors, continues to be at the forefront of the animal world's most serious and urgent matters. In May 2010, the partner organizations observed "Black and White Week," their campaign to draw attention to the plight of Tasmanian devils, whose distinct white strip on an otherwise black coat inspired the campaign's name. The endangered species, which Terri had been helping to save on the very day she learned of Steve's fateful accident, is dying off at an alarming rate from a highly contagious cancer known as devil facial tumor disease. To help raise awareness of the problem and funds toward a cure, the zoo held activities related to the Tasmanian devil at the zoo and continues to promote a public sponsorship program. Bindi, appropriately dressed in black and white stripes rather than khakis, helped lead a particularly special event of the week: a birthday celebration for the zoo's oldest devil, Jinki. "She's . . . seven years old, which is very exciting because it's unusual for devils to live that long," Bindi told *The Courier Mail*. She added that the birthday girl "can't actually have any cake," referring to the oversized banana-shaped treat that Bindi had the duty of carving. Other zoo missions continue in full force as well. The Australia Zoo Rescue Team works tirelessly for the oceans' sea turtles and other marine life. The zoo's state-of-the-art Australian Wildlife Hospital, inspired by Lyn Irwin and completed in 2008, takes in dozens of patients a day and offers daily public tours. Conservation programs and projects devoted to koalas, tigers, elephants, cheetahs, and, of course, crocodiles are going strong.

For wildlife lovers who want to be part of zoo happenings but just can't get there (or want more once they leave), Australia Zoo has a new solution. Australia Zoo TV, created in 2009, is the Irwins' latest way to bring their world right into people's homes. The Web-based network (at http://australiazoo.tv/) features eight channels, among them "Chat to a Keeper," "Daily Video Diaries," "Robert's Real Life Adventures," and "Australia Zoo Live." While the network is a great way to help zoo fans stay current, it also, poignantly, allows them to reminisce—on the Crocodile Hunter Channel, viewers can catch the one and only Steve Irwin in action any time.

SO MUCH MORE

In some ways, the little Irwin family of today is, naturally, differ-ent from the one Steve left. The baby boy whom he had just begun to guide is a young man, hosting his own wildlife Webisodes and bearing more of his dad's likeness by the day. The crocodile hunter's

Terri, Bindi, and Bob greet television host Oprah Winfrey at a tap-ing of her show in Sydney, Australia, on December 14, 2010.

wife, previously known by most as just that, is a crusader in her own right, helping lead some of the animal world's greatest battles as she raises two happy and independent children. Then there's the crocodile hunter's daughter, the once crimpy-pigtailed little girl who had waved goodbye like crazy, Terri described in *Steve & Me,* through a small airplane window in August 2006. Her father, silly and strong, stood atop his Ute (pickup truck) and enthusiastically waved back for what would be the very last time. The fluffy pigtails have long since gone the way of the little girl herself, replaced by sleek golden tresses that frame the pretty preteen's face. She's an actress, an author, a designer, and a role model. Woven into each hat she wears, though, is her truest passion. Bindi is, above all, the wildlife warrior Steve had never doubted she'd become.

That passion is where the family remains steadfast. In one of Terri's most recent interviews, she told *The Courier-Mail* (as reported by the Web site *Perth Now*) that she and the kids had sat down not long ago to discuss their goals. "There is so much more to us than just being a company," she said, presumably in reference to the empire that is Australia Zoo. "The more successful we can become the more we can put back into our important conservation projects." When the Irwins decided all those years ago to invite the world along with them, they knew what it was all for. Today, not as a husband and wife, but as a mum and the two children with whom she is "passionately in love," they know still.

In the wake of an unexpected loss, most people are left to rely on judgment as to what their loved one would wish of them. It's different for Steve Irwin's family and friends because in his case, there essentially is no question. In an interview featured on the DVD of his own memorial service, Steve, inadvertently and almost chillingly, offers the only advice his survivors will ever really need. "Anybody who has lost someone who is that close to you, you always carry that pain," he says, reflecting on the death of his own mum. "It hurts you, it devastates you forever, but you know what? You owe that person to get back up, and strive ahead, and try harder. . . . You gotta keep going."

How to Get Involved

The following organizations offer information and advice about how to get involved with conservation issues.

Australia Zoo Wildlife Warriors Worldwide
P.O. Box 29
Beerwah QLD 4519
Australia
http://www.wildlifewarriors.org.au
The Irwins' own partner organization offers a range of opportunities for anyone to help continue Steve's mission. A highlight for the youngest of warriors is the Joey Ambassador Program, which allows selected kids to spread the conservation message in special ways. Contact Wildlife Warriors Worldwide for details.

International Fund for Animal Welfare
290 Summer Street
Yarmouth Port, MA 02675
http://www.ifaw.org/ifaw_united_states
This group, based in Cape Cod, Massachusetts, is dedicated to helping all creatures great and small from the polar bears of Canada to aquatic birds threatened by the 2010 oil spill. Check its Web site for ways that people living anywhere can get involved.

Ocean Alliance
191 Weston Road
Lincoln, MA 01773
www.oceanalliance.org
Get involved with one of Terri and Bindi's most current and important causes: marine life conservation. Founded in 1971 in Massachusetts, Ocean Alliance believes that "conservation should be

a 'state of mind'"—and therefore makes education and outreach a major part of its mission.

Wildlife Conservation Society

2300 Southern Boulevard

Bronx, NY 10460

www.wcs.org

In the bustle of New York City, you will find a famous wildlife oasis that also serves as this organization's home base: the Bronx Zoo. Concerned with the conservation of both global natural habitats and urban wildlife parks, Wildlife Conservation Society offers an array of jobs, volunteer opportunities, and educational campaigns.

Student Conservation Association

689 River Road

P.O. Box 550

Charlestown, NH 03603

www.thesca.org

Headquartered in New Hampshire with offices nationwide, this organization exists solely to mobilize young people in the conservation movement. Countless internships are available in fields ranging from endangered species protection to wetlands preservation.

Chronology

1962	Stephen Robert Irwin is born to naturalists Bob and Lyn Irwin in Essendon, Victoria, Australia.
1970	The Irwins move to Beerwah, Queensland, where they begin work on what would soon become the Beerwah Reptile Park (officially opened in 1973).
1980	The Irwins change the name of their park to the Queensland Reptile and Fauna Park.
Late 1980s	Steve spends months alone in the Outback, catching crocodiles for the Queensland government.
1991	Steve meets Terri Raines at Australia Zoo.
1992	Steve and Terri marry in her hometown of Eugene, Oregon.
	Steve and Terri take over management (and half ownership) of the reptile park and rename it Australia Zoo.
1996	The Irwins' wildlife adventures (shot and produced by John Stainton) debut on Australian TV as *The Crocodile Hunter*.
Late 1990s	*The Crocodile Hunter* debuts in the United States (on Animal Planet) and dozens of other countries.
1998	Steve and Terri welcome their first child, Bindi Sue.
2000	Steve's beloved mum, Lyn, is killed in a car crash.
2002	Steve's film *Crocodile Hunter: Collision Course* opens in the United States.
	Steve starts the Steve Irwin Conservation Foundation, later renamed Australia Zoo Wildlife Warriors Worldwide.

2003	Australia Zoo unveils its 5,500-seat Crocoseum.
	The Irwins welcome their second child, Robert Clarence.
2004	Steve becomes the center of media scrutiny when he holds baby Bob during a crocodile demo.
2006	Steve is killed by a stingray off the Great Barrier Reef in Australia.
2007	*Bindi the Jungle Girl* debuts on Discovery Kids.
	Bindi launches clothing line, Bindi Wear International.
2008	Bindi becomes youngest person ever to win a Daytime Emmy Award.
	Bob Irwin leaves Australia Zoo.
	The Irwins launch Save Steve's Place campaign, an effort to prevent mining on the Steve Irwin Wildlife Reserve.
2009	Terri Irwin becomes an Australian citizen.
2010	DVD movie *Free Willy: Escape from Pirate's Cove*, starring Bindi, is released.
	Bindi and Random House Australia introduce the book series *Bindi Wildlife Adventures*.
	Australia Zoo celebrates its fortieth anniversary.

Glossary

aboriginal   In reference to a region's native peoples

apex predator   Any wild animal that kills and eats other animals, but is not prey itself; an animal at the top of the food chain

bauxite   A type of sedimentary rock that yields aluminum oxide, used to make a variety of products

charisma   A special charm or appeal

commercialize   To manage (or exploit) with the goal of personal profit

crocodilian   Any of an order of reptiles that includes crocodiles, alligators, and their living and extinct relatives

crusader   One who leads or takes part in an important, sometimes daring, project or undertaking

dinghy   A small rowboat or sailboat

documentary   A factual film or program

eco-friendly   The description of a product or practice that does not harm the earth or its resources ("green")

fauna   Animal life (especially as opposed to flora, or plant life)

freshwater crocodile   Any crocodile that lives in nonsalty waters, such as rivers

herpetology   The study of reptiles and amphibians

humpback whale   A type of large, endangered whale found in coastal waters. Humpback whales are known for their "songs"— characteristic moaning and howling sounds that carry through oceans.

marsupial   Any of an order of mammals that carry their young inside pouches on their bodies (e.g., kangaroos)

naturalist   One who studies any field of natural history, such as field biology

saltie   Any crocodile that lives in salt water; salties are the largest crocodilians on Earth.

Tasmanian devil   A carnivorous (meat-eating), nocturnal (day-sleeping) marsupial native to the Australian island of Tasmania; devils are about the size of badgers and have notably strong jaws.

Bibliography

"About Steve Irwin." Official Steve Irwin Day Web site. URL: http://www.steveirwinday.org/about/steve-irwin/. Accessed February 4, 2010.

"About Us!" Australia Zoo. URL: http://www.crocodilehunter.com.au/crocodile_hunter/about_steve_terri/about.html. Accessed May 7, 2010.

"Animal Planet Videos: The Crocodile Hunter Diaries: Bindi at Croc School." Animal Planet Web site, January 12, 2007. URL: http://animal.discovery.com/videos/the-crocodile-hunter-diaries-bindi-at-croc-school.html. Accessed May 21, 2010.

Ashby, Emily. "What Parents Need to Know: Bindi the Jungle Girl." Common Sense Media. URL: http://www.commonsensemedia.org/tv-reviews/bindi-jungle-girl. Accessed May 18, 2010.

Associated Press (AP). "'Crocodile Hunter' Steve Irwin killed by stingray." MSNBC, September 5, 2006. URL: http://www.msnbc.msn.com/id/14663786/. Accessed March 5, 2010.

"Australia Zoo Wildlife Warriors' Joey Ambassadors Set Loose for Steve Irwin Day!" Australia Zoo Wildlife Warriors, October 2, 2009. URL: http://www.steveirwinday.org/images/pdf/media-release-joey-ambassadors.pdf. Accessed February 2, 2010.

"Australia Zoo Wildlife Warriors—Australian Wildlife Hospital Celebrates One Year Anniversary." Australia Zoo Wildlife Warriors, November 12, 2009. URL: http://www.steveirwinday.org/images/pdf/media-release-one-year-hospital.pdf. Accessed June 2, 2010.

Australian Associated Press (AAP). "Irwin feared fast cars more than animals." NineMSN (Channel Nine News), September 10, 2006. URL: http://news.ninemsn.com.au/article.aspx?id=141770. Accessed May 18, 2010.

Australian Associated Press (AAP). "Irwin petition to 'Save Steve's Place.'" Sunshine Coast Daily, May 13, 2008. URL: http://www.sunshinecoastdaily.com.au/story/2008/05/13/irwin-petition-save-steves-place/. Accessed January 27, 2010.

Australian Associated Press (AAP). "Crikey! Snail named after Steve Irwin." ABC News (Australian Broadcasting Corporation), November 13, 2009. URL: http://www.abc.net.au/news/stories/2009/11/13/2742031 .htm. Accessed May 8, 2010.

Australian Associated Press (AAP). "Terri and Bindi Irwin take on Japanese whalers." *The Courier-Mail,* December 26, 2007. URL: http://www.couriermail.com.au/news/queensland/irwins-to-teach-whalers-a-lesson/story-e6freoof-1111115200600. Accessed February 3, 2010.

Australian Associated Press (AAP). "Terri denies plans to change Australia Zoo focus." *The Sydney Morning Herald,* March 18, 2008. URL: http://www.smh.com.au/news/people/terri-irwin-denies-plans-to-move-to-us/2008/03/18/1205602379447.html. Accessed May 27, 2010.

Baracaia, Alexa. "Tears of Crocodile Hunter's widow at TV awards." *London Evening Standard,* November 1, 2006. URL: http://www.thisislondon .co.uk/showbiz/article-23372655-tears-of-crocodile-hunters-widow-at-tv-awards.do. Accessed May 4, 2010.

Barber, Lynn. "'I'm not actually a birdwatcher.'" *The Observer* (UK), January 14, 2007. URL: http://www.guardian.co.uk/media/2007/jan/14/television .features. Accessed May 18, 2010.

Bennefield, Robin M. "Croc Hunter Live: In the Eye of the Storm." Animal Planet Fansite, June 10, 2003. URL: http://animal.discovery.com/fansites/crochunter/expedition/expedition.html. Accessed May 4, 2010.

"Bindi Irwin gear hits Vegas catwalks." *Herald Sun,* August 31, 2007. URL: http://www.news.com.au/business/bindi-irwin-gear-hits-vegas-catwalks/story-e6frfm1i-1111114308897. Accessed May 18, 2010.

"Bindi Irwin has the slime of her life as she wins two Nickelodeon Kids' Choice Award blimps!" Nickelodeon Australia, October 10, 2007. URL: http://www.xyznetworks.com.au/web/xyz/fileup/News/file/114 .pdf. Accessed June 1, 2010.

"Bindi Irwin Says G'Day to America." *Good Morning America* (online), January 21, 2007. URL: http://abcnews.go.com/GMA/story?id=2801283&page=1. Accessed May 18, 2010.

"Bindi Irwin Snags Emmy Nods." CBS News, June 13, 2008. URL: http://www.cbsnews.com/video/watch/?id=4179089n. Accessed May 28, 2010.

Bindi the Jungle Girl: Episodes. ABC (Australian Broadcasting Corporation) For Kids online. URL: http://www.abc.net.au/children/bindi/episodes.htm. Accessed May 26, 2010.

"Bindi: The Back Story." Video clips from Discovery Kids. URL: http://kids.discovery.com/tv/bindi/aboutBindi.html. Accessed January 27, 2010.

"Bindi's Say." Australia Zoo. URL: http://www.australiazoo.com.au/crocodile_hunter/about_steve_terri/bindi_say.html. Accessed January 27, 2010.

Bourke, Philippa. "Terri steps up to take over Steve's role of selling Australia." *The Sydney Morning Herald,* January 15, 2007. URL: http://www.smh.com.au/news/world/terris-selling-australia/2007/01/14/1168709615973.html. Accessed March 18, 2010.

"Brockovich joins fight to Save Steve's Place." Australia Zoo, August 17, 2009. http://www.savestevesplace.com/media/media-release-brockovich-joins-fight.pdf. Accessed June 1, 2010.

Brown, Anne-Louise. "Bindi Irwin helps pen book series." *Sunshine Coast Daily,* June 2, 2010. URL: http://www.sunshinecoastdaily.com.au/story/2010/06/02/how-wild-bindi-helps-pen-animal-book-series-irwin/. Accessed June 8, 2010.

Buchanan, Kathy. "Steve Irwin: The Full Story." *Reader's Digest* (Australia). URL: http://www.readersdigest.com.au/life/steve-irwin-the-full-story/article30581.html. Accessed March 4, 2010.

Burgess, Kelly. "Whale war controversy continues as authorities board Sea Shepherd vessel, seize items." *Los Angeles Times,* February 23, 2009. URL: http://latimesblogs.latimes.com/outposts/2009/02/whale-war.html. Accessed May 26, 2010.

Byrnes, Holly. "Russell Crowe fights for Steve's Irwin's wildlife reserve." *The Daily Telegraph,* April 21, 2009. URL: http://www.news.com.au/entertainment/movies/crowe-fights-for-irwin-on-us-tv/story-e6frfmvr-1225700459965. Accessed January 21, 2010.

"Chairman's Report 2009." Australia Zoo Wildlife Warriors Worldwide Limited, November 25, 2009. URL: http://wildlifewarriors.org.au/about_us/documents/ChairmansReport2009.pdf. Accessed May 7, 2010.

Clark, Champ. "Chip off the Old Croc." *People,* Vol. 67, No. 24, June 18, 2007. URL: http://www.people.com/people/archive/article/0,,20061188, 00.html. Accessed January 21, 2010.

"Crikey! The Bindi doll talks." *WA Today,* July 7, 2008. URL: http://www. watoday.com.au/lifestyle/crikey-the-bindi-doll-talks-20080707-32se .html. Accessed May 28, 2010.

"Crocodile Conservation." Australia Zoo Wildlife Warriors Worldwide Ltd. URL: http://www.wildlifewarriors.org.au/crocodile_conservation/ index.html. Accessed January 27, 2010.

"Crocodiles and Alligator Farms." American Alligator (Web site). URL: http://www.american-alligator.com/Crocodiles-and-Alligator-Farms .html. Accessed May 10, 2010.

Dalton, Trent, Matthew Fynes-Clinton, Glenis Green, Fiona Hudson, Michael Madigan, Melissa Maugeri, and John Wright. "Steve Irwin 1962 - 2006." *The Adelaide Advertiser,* September 8, 2006. URL: http:// www.adelaidenow.com.au/steve-irwin-1962-2006/story-e6frea6u- 1111112190359. Accessed February 2, 2010.

"'Destroy Irwin death tape before it gets out' - manager." MailOnline (*Daily Mail*), September 7, 2006. URL: http://www.dailymail.co.uk/ news/article-403924/Destroy-Irwin-death-tape-gets--manager.html. Accessed May 4, 2010.

Dick, Tim. "Irwin family rift? Crikey." *The Age,* March 21, 2008. Accessed May 8, 2010.

Duckett, Richard. "'I've got a gift, mate!'; croc hunter Steve Irwin doesn't mind if you think he's crazy." *Telegram & Gazette,* July 12, 2002. URL: http://proquest.umi.com/pqdweb?did=136110481&Fmt=3&clientId=81 634&RQT=309&VName=PQD. Accessed: February 4, 2010.

Elks, Sarah. "Mining ban campaign rejected." *The Australian,* December 29, 2009. URL: http://www.theaustralian.com.au/business/mining- energy/mining-ban-campaign-rejected/story-e6frg9df-1225814240130 ?from=public_rss. Accessed February 2, 2010.

"Exclusive: Bindi and Terri Irwin on Continuing 'Croc Hunter's' Legacy." *Good Morning America* (ABC News), December 8, 2006. URL: http:// abcnews.go.com/GMA/story?id=2710165. Accessed May 28, 2010.

"Father of the Man (Transcript)." *Australian Story* (Australian Broadcasting Corporation), April 7, 2008. URL: http://www.abc.net.au/austory/content/2007/s2210614.htm. Accessed June 2, 2010.

Field, Katherine (AAP). "Stars Come Out for Kids' Choice." *The Epoch Times,* November 12, 2009. URL: http://www.theepochtimes.com/n2/content/view/25156/. Accessed June 8, 2010.

Finn, Natalie. "Croc Hunter's Daughter Welcomed to the *Jungle.*" E! Online, October 16, 2006. URL: http://comcast.eonline.com/uberblog/b53541_croc_hunters_daughter_welcomed_jungle.html. Accessed May 4, 2010.

Gianficaro, Phil. "Boy is a boon to 4-legged pals." phillyBurbs.com, November 8, 2009. URL: http://www.phillyburbs.com/news/news_details/article/328/2009/november/08/boy-is-a-boon-to-4-legged-pals.html. Accessed May 28, 2010.

"Good Old Days!" Australia Zoo. URL: http://www.australiazoo.com.au/australia_zoo/good_old_days_new/good_old_days_main.htm. Accessed March 15, 2010.

"Govt to buy Cape York land for Irwin memorial reserve." Australian Broadcasting Corporation, July 22, 2007. URL: http://www.abc.net.au/news/stories/2007/07/22/1984870.htm. Accessed May 8, 2010.

Green, Glenis. "Better the devil you know and help to protect, says Bindi." *The Courier-Mail* (re-posted by Australia Zoo), May 17, 2010. URL: http://www.wildlifewarriors.org.au/in_the_media/. Accessed May 31, 2010.

Green, Glenis. "Terri Irwin would remarry for love." *The Courier-Mail* (posted by Perth Now), May 29, 2010. URL: http://www.perthnow.com.au/entertainment/terri-irwin-would-remarry-for-love/story-e6frg30c-1225872851590. Accessed June 3, 2010.

He Changed Our World: Steve Irwin Memorial Tribute. Hollywood: EMI America Records, 2006.

Hudson, Fiona, and Peter Hall. "Croc Hunter's dad Bob Irwin quits zoo." *Sunday Herald Sun,* March 2, 2008. URL: http://www.heraldsun.com.au/news/national/croc-hunters-dad-quits-zoo/story-e6frf7l6–1111115689002. Accessed June 4, 2010.

Hussey, Genevieve. "The Life and Times of Steve Irwin (Transcript)." *The 7:30 Report* (Australian Broadcasting Corporation), September 4, 2006. URL: http://www.abc.net.au/7.30/content/2006/s1732790.htm. Accessed: January 21, 2010.

"Interview with Crocodile Hunter Steve Irwin." *Scientific American* (online), March 26, 2001. URL: http://www.scientificamerican.com/article.cfm?id=interview-with-crocodile-2001–03. Accessed May 10, 2010.

"Interview with Steve Irwin (Transcript)." *Larry King Live* (CNN), November 25, 2004. URL: http://transcripts.cnn.com/TRANSCRIPTS/0411/25/lkl.01.html. Accessed January 27, 2010.

"Interview with Terri and Bindi Irwin, Widow and Daughter of Late Steve Irwin (Transcript)." *Larry King Live* (CNN), January 14, 2007. URL: http://transcripts.cnn.com/TRANSCRIPTS/0701/14/lkl.01.html. Accessed January 21, 2010.

"Irwin not backing down on bauxite mine." Australian Broadcasting Corporation (ABC News), May 13, 2008. URL: http://www.abc.net.au/news/stories/2008/05/13/2243680.htm. Accessed January 28, 2010.

Irwin, Steve & Terri. *The Crocodile Hunter: The Incredible Life and Adventures of Steve and Terri Irwin.* New York: Dutton, 2001.

Irwin, Terri. *Steve & Me* (large print edition). Waterville, Maine: Thorndike Press, 2008.

"It's Black and White." Australia Zoo News, May 9, 2010. URL: http://www.australiazoo.com/about-us/zoo-gossip/index.php?gossip=702. Accessed June 8, 2010.

Johnson, Ed. "Australian Stingrays Killed After Steve Irwin's Death." Bloomberg.com, September 13, 2006. URL: http://www.bloomberg.com/apps/news?pid=20601081&sid=acdQTOouT9rU. Accessed March 18, 2010.

Jones, Gemma. "Toy fair ban a croc: Bindi." *New York Post,* February 18, 2008. URL: http://www.nypost.com/p/news/regional/item_snOhLLQ RxoxATCsKCN0atM;jsessionid=5164D079334BE2FE5304D9F3BFA 91EEA. Accessed June 1, 2010.

Lalor, Peter, and Michael Bodey. "Obituary: Committed to lore of nature." *The Australian,* September 5, 2006. URL: http://www.theaustralian.com

.au/news/obituary-committed-to-lore-of-nature/story-e6frg6n6–1111112180984. Accessed May 4, 2010.

Lehmann, Megan. "How *Jungle Girl* Bindi Irwin Keeps Dad's Spirit Alive." *TV Guide,* June 8, 2007. URL: http://www.tvguide.com/news/jungle-girl-bindi-37790.aspx. Accessed May 28, 2010.

Leitch, Luke. "Life after Steve Irwin." *The Times,* October 25, 2007. URL: http://entertainment.timesonline.co.uk/tol/arts_and_entertainment/tv_and_radio/article2731174.ece. Accessed May 7, 2010.

"Lyn Irwin Memorial Fund." Australia Zoo. URL: http://www.crocodile hunter.com/conservation/lyn_irwin/index.html. Accessed March 15, 2010.

MacFarlane, Melanie. "Why Do Whales Beach Themselves"? G-Online, March 27, 2009. URL: http://www.gmagazine.com.au/features/1252/why-do-whales-beach-themselves?page=0%2C0. Accessed March 19, 2010.

Magann, Suzie. "Australia Zoo Blog: Steve Irwin Day 2009." Australia Zoo. URL: http://blogs.australiazoo.com.au/?p=2451. Accessed June 7, 2010.

Mann, Simon. "Planet Irwin." *The Age,* September 9, 2006. URL: http://www.theage.com.au/news/in-depth/planet-irwin/2006/09/08/1157222329640.html?page=fullpage#contentSwap2. Accessed March 15, 2010.

Marks, Kathy. "Irwin's fans take out grief in 'revenge attacks' on stingrays." *The Independent,* September 13, 2006. URL: http://www.independent.co.uk/news/world/australasia/irwins-fans-take-out-grief-in-revenge-attacks-on-stingrays-415750.html. Accessed June 2, 2010.

McGlone, Julie. "Swinging with the Jungle Girl." *Jetstar Magazine* (Asia Edition), July 2008. URL: http://www.jetstarmag.com/story/swinging-with-the-jungle-girl/397/1/. Accessed February 3, 2010.

McMahon, Barbara. "Father of crocodile man Steve Irwin quits zoo in family row." *The Guardian,* March 3, 2008. URL: http://www.guardian.co.uk/world/2008/mar/03/Australia. Accessed May 26, 2010.

Mitchell, Peter. "Terri hits out at Bindi critics." *The Sunday Times,* January 14, 2007. URL: http://www.perthnow.com.au/entertainment/

terri-hits-out-at-bindi-critics/story-e6frg30c-1111112833116. Accessed February 3, 2010.

"Mountain gorillas named in traditional Rwandan ceremony." The Gorilla Organization, July 2, 2007. URL: http://www.gorillas.org/gorilla_ naming_2007. Accessed June 1, 2010.

Murdoch, Anna King. "He's smart, by crikey." *The Age,* June 10, 2003. URL: http://www.theage.com.au/articles/2003/06/09/1055010919523 .html. Accessed August 25, 2010.

Murray, Rebecca. "'Croc Hunter - Collision Course' Interview." About .com: Hollywood Movies, July 2002. URL: http://movies.about.com/ library/weekly/aa070502a.htm. Accessed March 18, 2010.

"Obituaries: Steve Irwin." *The Independent,* September 5, 2006. URL: http://www.independent.co.uk/news/obituaries/steve-irwin-414682 .html. Accessed February 11, 2010.

Oregon State University. "Oregon State University Gets Grant from Irwins to Study Whales." Salem-News.com, January 8, 2008. URL: http://www.salem-news.com/articles/january082008/osu_irwins_ whales_010808.php. Accessed May 28, 2010.

"Our Books: Bindi Wildlife Adventures." Random House Australia. URL: http://www.randomhouse.com.au/Books/Default.aspx?Page=Bo ok&ID=9781864719963. Accessed June 8, 2010.

Perry, Beth. "The Green Party." *People,* Vol. 67, No. 15, April 16, 2007. URL: http://www.people.com/people/archive/article/0,,20061873,00 .html. Accessed June 2, 2010.

"Planet's Best with Terri and Bindi: Terri Irwin." Animal Planet Web site. URL: http://animal.discovery.com/tv/planets-best/terri-bindi/terri- bindi_02.html. Accessed May 7, 2010.

"Q&A with Bindi Irwin." *J-14,* April 1, 2010. URL: http://www.j-14 .com/2010/04/qa-with-bindi-irwin.html. Accessed May 27, 2010.

"Radio Broadcasts from the Club: Terri and Bindi Irwin." National Press Club Online, July 14, 2007. URL: http://www.press.org/activities/ programs/xmradio/20070714_Irwins.mp3. Accessed: February 2, 2010.

"Reptiles: Alligator & Crocodile." San Diego Zoo Web site. URL: http://www .sandiegozoo.org/animalbytes/t-crocodile.html. Accessed May 19, 2010.

Rivera, Larry. "Steve Irwin - Crocodile Hunter." About.com, Australia/ New Zealand Travel. http://goaustralia.about.com/od/knowthepeople/ a/steveirwin.htm?r=et. Accessed March 16, 2010.

Robson, Frank. "Crikey, it's raw Stevo!" *The Good Weekend,* April 2002 (reprinted in *The Sydney Morning Herald,* September 4, 2006). URL: http://www.smh.com.au/articles/2006/09/04/1157222053963.html. Accessed February 4, 2010.

Robson, Lou. "Crikey! Now Bindi Wins an Emmy." *Sunday Herald Sun,* June 15, 2008. URL: http://www.heraldsun.com.au/entertainment/ tv/crikey-now-bindi-wins-an-emmy/story-e6frf9ho-1111116636667. Accessed May 21, 2010.

Sea Shepherd Conservation Society. "The *Steve Irwin* Departs for Antarctica." Sea Shepherd News, December 7, 2009. URL: http://www .seashepherd.org/news-and-media/news-091207-1.html. Accessed February 4, 2010.

"Sea Shepherd vessel named in honour of Steve Irwin." *Shipping Times,* December 6, 2007. URL: http://www.shippingtimes.co.uk/item998_ steve_irwin.htm. Accessed May 26, 2010.

Siddique, Haroon. "Japanese whaling boat clash likely to ignite row over activists' tactics." *The Guardian,* January 6, 2010. URL: http://www .guardian.co.uk/environment/2010/jan/06/japan-whaling-sea- shepherd-greenpeace. Accessed May 26, 2010.

"Sir David Attenborough." British Broadcasting Company (BBC), 2008. URL: http://www.bbc.co.uk/nature/programmes/who/david_ attenborough.shtml. Accessed May 21, 2010.

"Steve and Terri Irwin (Transcript)." *Enough Rope with Andrew Denton* (Australian Broadcasting Corporation), March 22, 2004. URL: http:// www.abc.net.au/tv/enoughrope/transcripts/s1071026.htm. Accessed June 1, 2010.

"Steve Irwin Gets His Way." *The Courier-Mail,* January 2, 2007. URL: http://www.couriermail.com.au/news/queensland/steve-irwin-gets-his- way/story-e6freoof-1111112773525. Accessed June 1, 2010.

"Steve Irwin Show Opens Day's Events." Australian Football Association of North America, January 16, 2006. URL: http://www.afana.com/drupal5/news/2006/09/04/steve_irwin_dies_tragic_accident-238. Accessed May 13, 2010.

"Steve Irwin." Encyclopedia of World Biography. URL: http://www.notablebiographies.com/supp/Supplement-Fl-Ka/Irwin-Steve.html. Accessed March 18, 2010.

"Terri Irwin (Transcript)." *Enough Rope with Andrew Denton* (Australian Broadcasting Corporation), October 29, 2007. URL: http://www.abc.net.au/tv/enoughrope/transcripts/s2073025.htm. Accessed May 30, 2010.

"Terri Irwin Citizenship Ceremony." ImmiTV (Australian Government Department of Immigration and Citizenship), December 8, 2009. URL: http://www.youtube.com/watch?v=Irkr51Ph4us. Accessed May 27, 2010.

"Terri Irwin Live Chat Archive." MSN and Animal Planet, 2001. URL: http://animal.discovery.com/fansites/crochunter/chat_archive.html. Accessed March 18, 2010.

"The Crocodile Hunter: Steve Irwin Talks to Scholastic News." Scholastic News Online, September 5, 2006 (originally printed April 2002). URL: http://www2.scholastic.com/browse/article.jsp?id=7401. Accessed February 12, 2010.

"Trapping Crocodiles." Australia Zoo. URL: http://www.crocodilehunter.com.au/crocodile_hunter/trapping.html. Accessed March 15, 2010.

Vickers, Lucy. "Khaki-clad kids save wildlife." *The North Shore Times,* October 29, 2009. URL: http://www.stuff.co.nz/auckland/local-news/north-shore-times/3007021/Khaki-clad-kids-save-wildlife. Accessed January 27, 2010.

"Visit to Australia Zoo, Queensland (Home of The Croc Hunter, Steve Irwin!!!)." Gavin's Weblog, December 29, 2005. URL: http://www.x2gav.co.uk/?p=20. Accessed May 8, 2010.

Whiting, Frances. "Terri fights to halt croc eggs harvest." *The Sunday Mail,* June 10, 2007 (re-posted by Australia Zoo). URL: http://

www.australiazoo.com.au/about-us/in-the-news/index.php?month= 06&year=2007. Accessed: May 10, 2010.

"Wild Animals A–Z: Crocodile." Animal Planet Web site. URL: http:// animal.discovery.com/reptiles/crocodile/. Accessed May 19, 2010.

Wynhausen, Elisabeth. "Now that he's gone." *The Australian,* November 3, 2007. URL: http://www.theaustralian.com.au/news/features/now-that-hes-gone/story-e6frg8h6–1111114786763. Accessed May 5, 2010.

Further Resources

Baker, Trevor. *Steve Irwin: The Incredible Life of the Crocodile Hunter.* New York: Thunders Mouth Press, 2006.

Bekstrom-Guthrie, Sheryl. *Crocodile Tears: The Larger Than Life Story of Steve Irwin, the Crocodile Hunter.* West Conshohocken, PA: Infinity Publishing, 2009.

Irwin, Steve & Terri. *The Crocodile Hunter: The Incredible Life and Adventures of Steve and Terri Irwin.* New York: Dutton, 2001.

Irwin, Terri. *Steve & Me.* New York: Gallery Books (a division of Simon & Schuster), 2008.

Lynch, Peter. *Wildlife & Conservation Volunteering: The Complete Guide.* Chalfont St. Peter, Bucks, UK: Bradt Travel Guides, 2009.

Primack, Richard B. *A Primer of Conservation Biology, Fourth Edition.* Sunderland, MA: Sinauer Associates, Inc., 2008.

Shears, Richard. *Wildlife Warrior: Steve Irwin: 1962–2006, a Man Who Changed the World.* Chatswood, New South Wales: New Holland Publishers Australia, 2006.

WEB SITES

Defenders of Wildlife Kids' Planet

www.kidsplanet.org

The Washington, D.C.-based conservation organization Defenders of Wildlife offers a special resource just for students. This site features fact sheets, games, ideas for getting involved and more.

The National Geographic Society

www.nationalgeographic.com

National Geographic has been the authority on the natural world for more than a century. Find facts on animals listed from A to Z among other features on the society's Web site.

U.S. Fish and Wildlife Service Endangered Species Program

http://www.fws.gov/endangered

Countless animal species are increasingly threatened every day by human interference and other factors. Learn all about the world of endangered species, from those in faraway countries to ones virtually in your own backyard. Click "For Kids" for special student resources.

Picture Credits

Index

133

About the Author

AMY E. BREGUET is a freelance writer and editor with a special interest in the educational value of pop culture. A graduate of the Mass Communication program at Westfield State College in Westfield, Massachusetts, she worked at a daily newspaper and an educational publishing company before shifting to a freelance career. Breguet lives in Southampton, Massachusetts, with her husband Charlie and children Hope, Casey, and Joseph.